MY
RESCUE
PET
Rescued Me

MY RESCUE PET RESCUED ME

An Hachette UK Company
www.hachette.co.uk

Summersdale Publishers Ltd
Part of Octopus Publishing Group Limited
Carmelite House
50 Victoria Embankment
LONDON
EC4Y 0DZ
UK

www.summersdale.com

Printed and bound by CPI Group (UK) Ltd, Croydon, CR0 4YY

ISBN: 978-1-78783-986-1

Substantial discounts on bulk quantities of Summersdale books are available to corporations, professional associations and other organizations. For details contact general enquiries: telephone: +44 (0) 1243 771107 or email: enquiries@summersdale.com.

MY RESCUE PET

Rescued Me

Amazing True Stories of Adopted Animal Heroes

Sharon Ward Keeble

summersdale

To all the amazing animal rescuers who open their lives and their hearts to the unwanted and the unloved. Thank you for everything you do to give these precious creatures a chance. There are few things more rewarding than the unconditional love of a rescue pet and I am grateful that there are so many humans who care.

About the Author

Sharon Ward Keeble is a journalist with more than 30 years' experience of international reporting for major women's magazines and news sites in the UK, USA and Australia, including *Closer*, *Bella*, *Take a Break*, the *Daily Mail*, *That's Life* and *New Idea*. She is the author of *My Rescue Dog Rescued Me* and the memoir *China: Passport to Adventure* as well as the co-author of *The Horse Girl*. She is based in Florida with her own pets – four dogs and a Hemingway cat named Ernest.

Contents

10   Introduction

13   Chapter 1: **Alesha and Zeppy the Dog**

19   Chapter 2: **Jodie and Easter the Turkey**

31   Chapter 3: **Christine and Mickey the Cat**

39   Chapter 4: **Gaby and Mo the Dog**

47   Chapter 5: **Ahnya and Lucky the Cat**

54   Chapter 6: **Faith and Micco the Dog**

63   Chapter 7: **Lauren and the Guinea Pigs Constantine and Crystal**

71   Chapter 8: **Kim and Charley the Dog**

79   Chapter 9: **Carla and Daniel the Duck**

90   Chapter 10: **Taylor and Duke the Dog**

99   Chapter 11: **Nina and Tracy the Lemur**

108   Chapter 12: **Gina and Alex the Tiger**

117   Chapter 13: **Hazel and Bob the Dog**

125   Chapter 14: **Luana and Nurse Zulu the Cat**

132   Chapter 15: **Lisette and Beautie the Three-Legged Dog**

139   Chapter 16: **Hannah and Blu the Budgie**

146   Chapter 17: **David and Jess the Dog**

152   Chapter 18: **Melanie and the Rescue Pigs**

162   Chapter 19: **Rachel and the Dogs Patty and Bonnie**

170   Chapter 20: **Helen and Russell the Crow**

177   Chapter 21: **Alex and Mortimer the Guinea Pig**

185   Chapter 22: **Laura and Angel the Horse**

195   Chapter 23: **Angela and Capone the Dog**

200   Chapter 24: **Hesther and Black the Donkey**

208   Chapter 25: **Annie and Cherry the Horse**

215   Chapter 26: **Tiffany and Angel the Dog**

223   Chapter 27: **Nicky and Spare the Cat**

230   Chapter 28: **Tracey and Scout the Dog**

238   Chapter 29: **Amanda and Piper Paws the Cat**

243   Chapter 30: **Marthe and Peggy the Dog**

251   Afterword

253   Rescue Pet Resources

255   Acknowledgements

Introduction

Rescue animals have been a central part of my family throughout my life – and particularly after I had my three children. We have given a loving home to bunnies, hamsters, three rescue dogs and even, at one point, a bird. I guess my husband David and I could never ever say no to a pet in need.

I always knew that they were all special in their own right, but after I wrote my book *My Rescue Dog Rescued Me*, I wanted to explore the effects other animals have had on their human rescuers.

Researching this book was exciting and inspiring as, time and again, I heard stories of many different animals who have had the most amazing, positive effect on the lives of their humans.

When you read this book, you will discover the incredible story of Alex, the tiger who kept his friend Gina from a lonely life of drug addiction. There is Daniel, the duck who saved his owner Carla more than once when she spiralled into a deep depression and PTSD after a life-changing accident. There's also Mickey, the feral cat who helped his owner deal with the loss of her son in a terrorist attack, and Angel, the horse who inspired the creation of a rescue centre for other animals in need.

You will also read a story very personal to me: Micco, the rescued German shepherd pup who has truly made a huge difference to my 13-year-old daughter Faith's life as she copes with watching her dad Dave battle motor neuron disease.

In every true story, I learned that all of these rescue animals have so much to give regardless of their backgrounds. They provide emotional and physical support when it's needed the most, and their love is unconditional.

Personally, my family has learned some important life lessons thanks to our big-hearted rescues. They have taught us all how to be more giving and non-judgmental, and how to love freely.

There are too many animals in this world who need a good home through no fault of their own. My wish is that this book will encourage everyone to consider opening their hearts to these special creatures who inevitably change our lives so much for the better.

Chapter 1

ALESHA AND ZEPPY THE DOG

It was a cool July day in Minot, North Dakota, when Alesha picked up the miniature dachshund she had agreed to foster. She had heard about the sweet little guy through a friend and thought Zeppy would make a wonderful companion for her own rescue dog Miley back home in Sioux Falls, South Dakota.

A shelter had saved Zeppy from abusive owners who had badly beaten him. Sadly, his foster mom was moving and couldn't take him with her, so Alesha stepped in. As it happened, she was in town delivering flowers for her work anyway, so could collect her new charge at the same time.

As soon as Zeppy met her, he jumped on her lap and licked her face, which was astonishing because he suffered from extreme anxiety and wasn't always good with strangers.

"I fell in love with Zeppy as soon as we met," recalls Alesha. "He was so friendly and happy to see me. His foster parent was sorry to see him go but relieved when she saw how delighted he was to meet me. I couldn't wait to get him home to meet Miley. I felt so sure that they would get on."

The summer had been particularly wet and rainy in Minot. The snow had been late in thawing and then there had been strong storms that produced a lot of rain. It had been wet for days and parts of Minot were flooded, so the National Guard had been drafted in to keep people safe by barricading the roads that were impassable.

Alesha decided to drive home to Sioux Falls at 4 a.m. to avoid the traffic. Being so early, it was pitch black and she had to turn around and take a detour when one of the main roads she needed to take was cordoned off. She carried on and came to another blockade at a dip in the road. There were no National Guard present to turn the traffic around.

Alesha watched as another car drove through the rising water. Because she was in a big truck, Alesha thought she must be safe to continue her drive down this particular stretch of road. As she drove into the water-filled dip, the truck started to spin out of control. Thinking fast, she grabbed her phone and put her foot down on the brake to steady the vehicle.

She still doesn't know how far they spun into the water, but eventually the tyres caught on a ledge or a rock and the spinning stopped. But, by this time, the waters were rising and flooding into the truck. The cab filled with freezing cold water right up to her chest and it all happened so fast that there was little she could do. Poor Zeppy was screaming with fear, but with Alesha's help he made it onto her chest, where he stayed with her arms wrapped safely around him.

So there Alesha was, her leg stretched out as far as she could to keep her foot on the brake, one arm around the dog and, like this, she somehow managed to get through to the emergency services.

For the longest hour and a half of her life, she waited to be rescued with just five inches of air in the truck, not knowing if she and Zeppy could survive or whether they would be swept out into the nearby river.

"When I called nine-one-one, I must have sounded hysterical because the woman couldn't understand me," says Alesha. "I tried to be calm but I was terrified. I was so cold I couldn't feel my body but I was aware that my foot needed to stay on that brake if we stood any chance of surviving the flood waters. Sweet Zeppy, although initially he was shaking with the cold and whimpering with fear, clung to my chest and stayed surprisingly calm. The feeling of his warm body on my chest consoled me but it was also very sobering because I knew I had to remain level-headed if we were to survive. It wasn't just my life at stake but his, too."

It seemed like forever until Alesha heard the sound and saw the lights of the rescue boat. They were looking for her but it was so dark and murky that they couldn't see her. She screamed for help but it felt like no one heard her. Zeppy barked hard as they came closer, but still the boat seemed to be going away from them.

In desperation, she dunked Zeppy under the water and out of the truck window in the hope he would keep barking and swim toward the boat. Amazingly, he did just that and the rescue squad saw him. Minutes later, they were both pulled into the boat and, as Alesha was dragged from the truck, it floated off down the road.

"I know it sounds horrible, but I couldn't think what else to do," says Alesha. "Zeppy was going crazy barking, so I grabbed his harness and dunked him in the water. The little guy kept on swimming and barking and his voice was heard. If it hadn't been for his bravery, we might not be here today. I had no idea if he would carry on barking – I just had to put my faith in him. I may have rescued him, but he definitely rescued me right back that day!"

Alesha suffered severe hypothermia and temporarily lost some of the feeling in her legs due to the cold. But it was the fear that bothered her more than anything. For three days she couldn't close her eyes because she could see herself spinning out of control in the deep waters. Even when she did drift off to sleep, her dreams were nightmares, so her doctor gave her anxiety medicine and she was eventually diagnosed with severe post-traumatic stress disorder.

Her recovery wasn't easy, but it was during these traumatic times that she and Zeppy bonded. He would sit up with her in the night when she couldn't sleep or she woke up from another nightmare. He would lie down on her lap for hours and wouldn't leave her. Sometimes, when he slept, he would whimper and Alesha wondered if he was suffering from scary dreams, too, so she would snuggle him in closer to her and hold him tight. They formed an extreme bond and unquestionably helped each other. As the months went by, the nightmares grew less intense and the two survivors started to get their lives back to some kind of normality. If it hadn't been for the love of her foster Zeppy and, of course, her rescue pup Miley, Alesha says she would never have come to terms with what happened to her.

Miley, another miniature dachshund, was Alesha's "sober dog", so called because, after she won a long ten-year battle with addiction to meth and painkillers in 2009, Alesha adopted her as an 11-week-old puppy from a local barn. It had turned out that Miley was the best thing to have happened to Alesha. Not only were they close, but she kept Alesha occupied enough to keep her drug-free. The two were also inseparable and, after the accident, Miley was always around to cheer Alesha up and cuddle her when she needed it the most. Miley also took Zeppy in as if she knew that they were kindred spirits, both needing Alesha and a loving home.

A couple of summers after the accident, Alesha, who had always been an outdoors girl, was still terrified of going near water and was even scared if it started to rain. Her doctor suggested she go kayaking. At first, she thought it was a crazy idea until she spoke with a friend, who agreed to go with her.

To make it easier and to give her confidence, she took along Miley. Her dog also did not like the water and Alesha thought they could support each other to get over their phobias. They managed less than an hour in the kayak.

Both girls were shaking and Alesha had flashbacks of the truck spinning out of control, but together they managed it.

It took several attempts to feel comfortable but now Alesha, Miley and sometimes Zeppy go kayaking together and it's become one of Miley's favourite pastimes. Together, they have kayaked well over 400 river miles – not bad for the pair who once hated water.

Alesha is now an animal activist who works for several shelters near her home in Minnesota. She goes to houses to pick up unwanted animals and helps find them homes or foster parents. It is work that she is passionate about, fuelled by her own successes with rescues in the shape of Zeppy and Miley.

"I have no doubt that Zeppy saved my life that day," says Alesha. "Really, we didn't even know each other but the warmth of his body on my chest and the selfless way he swam out to get help was above and beyond. I don't want children and so my dogs – and all the dogs I rescue – are my babies, who I adore. My PTSD is definitely better and I can talk about the incident now, but I am also still drug-free – a major achievement. I put a large part of my success down to my dogs. They have always given me a lot to be grateful for and every day spent with them is a joy. I'm a lucky girl, that's for sure!"

Chapter 2

JODIE AND EASTER THE TURKEY

When Jodie met Jerry, her boss at the internet service provider where they both worked, she was already in a long-term relationship. Jerry was the cool guy, a fantastic leader and an intelligent man who everyone respected and adored, including Jodie.

In 2008, when America hit a recession, Jodie got laid off from the job she loved, along with many other people from her company. She was devastated and the loss of her position had a serious impact on her life. She suffered from severe anxiety and depression, but her boyfriend wasn't supportive and it was Jerry she turned to for emotional support. He would check in on Jodie most days and take her out for lunch with some of her old co-workers. He made her feel that she was worthy again and she realized that losing her job wasn't anything personal – she was, unfortunately, just another casualty of the recession.

When she split up with her boyfriend, it was again Jerry who she went to for advice and support. She was a damsel in distress and he was her knight in shining armour who won her over with care and attention.

One day, during a lunch date, Jerry admitted that he had romantic feelings for her and she realized that for weeks she had felt the same.

"I was head over heels in love with that man," recalls Jodie. "He swept me off my feet and he was there when I needed someone the most. I think the fact he was a few years older was very attractive to me, plus he was loved and respected by everyone in the workplace. I couldn't believe he would choose me! He was also incredibly supportive of me, particularly when I felt down or wrestled with anxiety. I knew very early on that he was the man I wanted to spend the rest of my life with."

The couple moved in together, and when Jerry's company announced more people would be laid off, they took advantage and moved from Salt Lake City in Utah to Washington state to be closer to Jerry's family.

A year later, on Valentine's Day 2011, they eloped. It was a small ceremony in a registry office, which was followed in the summer by a much larger celebration that they held on the property they had bought in the countryside.

It was a beautiful day as they said "I do" for the second time, in the woods at the back of their dream home, a cabin, and it looked like Jodie had it all. She had a husband she loved and a beautiful home, but already cracks were beginning to show in their relationship.

"Jerry had become very controlling of me," says Jodie. "I couldn't go out on my own without his say so. At first, I liked the fact that he cared so much but then it became too much, and I resented it. He was also often dismissive of me – whatever I said was always wrong – and he developed an angry attitude, like everything I did annoyed him. Sometimes I was scared to say anything for fear of being put down. He refused to have marriage counselling but I did have personal therapy. Jerry had always said that our issues were caused by my own problems, so I blamed myself for a while. But honestly, the damage had been done to our relationship and I was desperately unhappy."

Feeling alone and unsupported, Jodie didn't know what to do. She built a little wooden shelter in the woods where she would go for time out from Jerry, and that became her only escape. But little did she know that help was on its way in the form of a tiny, two-week-old turkey chick.

It was April 2014, and Jodie and Jerry had invited a couple of friends over for dinner to celebrate Easter. On the way, they saw an adorable little yellow and black chick abandoned at the side of the road. It was so small they almost drove past it but, having noticed a flash of colour, they stopped.

When the guests arrived at the house with a bottle of wine and the chick in a coffee can, Jodie's heart flipped.

"The chick wouldn't stop staring at me," recollects Jodie. "It was as if her eyes were cutting into my soul, the look was so intense. I gently picked her up and she sat in my hands, very peaceful and quiet. I knew there and then that I wanted to keep her. Although it sounds a bit unhinged, something inside me told me that she needed to stay with me. It was such a strong feeling and I can't explain it except that I had a very clear image in my mind of this sweet little turkey chick coming with me in my car, sleeping in my bedroom and of us walking around the property together. I couldn't let her go. She was mine."

Jodie had no experience with looking after birds, so she did some online research into how to raise a turkey. She called the chick Easter and, against Jerry's wishes, she let it roam around their home; she would not be without her new pet.

By this point, their relationship was at a critical low and Jodie was sleeping on the sofa, only now with Easter in her makeshift bed, made out of a box, beside her. Turkeys are very sociable creatures and, at first, Easter would keep Jodie up all night with her chirps as she lay alone in her warming box. She was crying because she wanted to sleep with Jodie and, as soon as she let Easter curl up in the crook of her arm or on her shoulder to sleep, the chirping stopped and they both slept like babies.

It was during these early days on the sofa that Easter and Jodie bonded. After a good night's sleep, Easter would follow Jodie into the bedroom, where she would return to dress, or she would squeeze into Jodie's bathrobe to keep warm. She particularly enjoyed running around with Jodie's three cats, who took to Easter as much as she fell in love with them. It was an unlikely friendship but nevertheless wonderful to witness.

"Those early days were the best," says Jodie. "I didn't like sleeping on the sofa on my own, so when Easter arrived I wasn't lonely any more. If I woke up in the middle of the night, she would be snuggled up right against me and I felt safe somehow. I am certain that she imprinted on me, meaning that she bonded with me so much that she believed that I was her mother. Being so close from such an early age and me letting her sleep with me on the sofa solidified her feelings for me. I loved her like a mom loves her baby and she became my trusted companion who rarely left my side unless I went to work and she stayed at home."

On the day of their July wedding anniversary, when Easter was three months old, Jerry asked Jodie for a divorce. That same night, he told Jodie that Easter couldn't stay in the house any more because he was tired of the mess and Easter had to live out on the porch. After an argument, Jodie reluctantly put Easter and her box outside, but that night she was attacked by a possum, which tore into her chest and broke a wing. Jodie woke up to her anguished cries and she was devastated when she found her barely alive.

Jodie lay next to her on the floor as Easter stared at her, panic-stricken and gasping for breath, with blood all over her chest and the floor. Jerry said she would be okay, but Jodie knew that if she didn't get help, her beloved turkey would die. She found an old fruit box and wrapped Easter in a blanket before she told Jerry that she was taking some of their savings to pay for any medical treatment Easter might need. Even if Jerry had said no, Jodie was determined to make sure her pet survived.

Jodie raced to the veterinary surgery with Easter bleeding in her lap. "Hang in there, hang in there," she told Easter over and over again between frantic sobs, as she willed her to survive long enough to make it to the vet's, where she had a chance of living.

As she had suffered severe blood loss and was in shock, Easter really should have died that day but, miraculously, the vet managed to stabilize her. She may have lost half her wing and would go on to spend four days at the vet's practice, but she was alive and that was all that mattered.

By the time Easter was six months old and she had grown into a beautiful Broad Breasted Bronze turkey – which are famous for being the official Thanksgiving turkey in America – she and Jerry lived apart, although divorce proceedings had not yet begun. Jodie was left alone with Easter and the cats. According to her, if it hadn't been for Easter, she wouldn't have survived the upset of the separation.

"When I was with Easter, I felt only joy," says Jodie. "I could come home from work after a bad day or an argument with Jerry and she would be there waiting for me. As soon as she heard me, she would chirp loudly, as if she were welcoming me home. No matter how bad the day, she made me smile without fail. I would hug my 'turkey girl' tight and she would let me. Despite everything, I was devastated with the breakdown of my marriage, but with her by my side I knew I would make it, because she was my support."

Together, Jodie and Easter took on the world. One of Jodie's jobs was as a performer as a fire-eater and she would take Easter with her in the car when she had her shows. The turkey would sit in the passenger seat and doze, scratch her head or watch the scenery go by. Easter was the perfect travelling companion, and if Jodie ever felt anxious, she would just rest her hand on Easter's back and she felt safe.

They clocked up thousands of miles on their road trips and everyone who met Easter loved her. She was a talking point, garnering a lot of attention from strangers who were fascinated with her. And Easter lapped it up.

Jodie stayed in touch with Jerry, despite everything, and when he called her crying one day in May 2015, she knew that something terrible had happened. He had been diagnosed with stage four oesophageal cancer and had been given just months to live. He'd been ill on and off for a few months with problems swallowing, but no one could have prepared him for the news that he was dying.

One of the first things Jerry did after he told Jodie the news was to start the divorce process. It proved very traumatic for Jodie because, deep down, she still loved the handsome man who had won her heart all those years ago, despite his flaws.

"I found the divorce procedure very unsettling and dealing with that and the news of Jerry's serious illness was too much," recalls Jodie. "Part of me felt that I had failed again in life, like I did when I lost my job all those years ago. I would come home in tears and immediately call for Easter, who would come waddling, shouting loudly.

She was always so delighted to see me and I knew she could sense I was upset. I would sit and talk to her and she would cluck as if she understood what I was going through, telling me that, no matter what, she was never going to leave. Easter knew exactly what was going on with her mommy and she wanted to help in the only way she knew how – by showing me how deeply she loved me. She would peck at my fingernails to say hello and then follow me everywhere, never letting me out of her sight. At night, a time when things seemed so much worse, she was my constant and I relied on her company."

The day Jerry passed away was one of the worst days of Jodie's life. A friend called to break the news and she pulled over to the side of the road and sobbed. To make matters worse for Jodie, she and Jerry had just recently signed the divorce papers but, as he had passed away before a judge could ratify them, she was technically left a widow.

At the time, Jodie was renting a room in a house and all the grief from her divorce and from Jerry's death came to a head. She became depressed and some days she couldn't even get out of bed. She was left with the task of going to their dream home, which was up for sale, and bagging the clothes and possessions that he had left behind. It was a deeply moving task that signalled the end of a huge chapter in her life. Her therapist called it complicated grief and, given all her mixed-up feelings, it was difficult to handle.

"I was left with an empty cabin and just a bunch of memories, many of them painful," says Jodie. "Many times,

Easter would see me crying on the couch, jump onto my lap and rest her head in my arm as if to say, 'It's okay, Mom, I'm here now, everything will be fine.' I was a wreck, filled with thoughts of failure, what-ifs and whether I would ever be happy again. My grief was complicated – even though Jerry had dumped me, I still had feelings for him, rightly or wrongly. I couldn't help it. When I couldn't get out of bed, Easter would scratch at the blankets with her beak, peck at my hands to get me to move and then scratch her head, which was another way to get my attention. I quickly realized that I had to get up and make an effort for Easter's sake. By focusing on her needs, she brought me from a very dark place and put me back together. For a long time, she was the only bright spot in my life, and without her I couldn't have carried on."

Jodie and Easter moved into a mobile home in Oregon, where she thought she might escape her grief, and it certainly helped. Easter became a bit of a local celebrity with her neighbours, who waved when she and Jodie went for walks. One was a lonely old man who lived across the street. He had a heart of gold and Easter would trot across to see him and make him laugh as if she knew that he needed company sometimes.

Having Easter forced Jodie to interact with people and get out of the house – the turkey was such a talking point and she led Jodie to new, lasting friendships as she slowly healed. While she rebuilt her life with Easter by her side, Jodie visited family in Salt Lake City. Being with Jerry had kept her isolated from her family and she hadn't seen many of them in years. Going home for the first time in a long time for Christmas 2015 entailed getting on a plane and, given her anxiety, Jodie didn't think that she could go until someone suggested taking Easter along for the ride as a service pet. She was such a good car passenger – why not take her on a plane?

Her therapist had certified Easter as a genuine emotional-support animal, so Jodie was able to show her papers to the airline. The airline agreed and Easter became possibly the first turkey to fly with passengers in America. Jodie made her a little kennel to wheel her through the airport, but she was allowed out on a leash while in flight, much to the delight of the cabin crew, who took her into the cockpit to meet the captain.

Easter flew four times and each time she made friends along the way. She brought so much joy to the people she met, who were amazed at how little fuss she caused and how sociable she was – Easter could get a smile out of anyone!

"She loved being in the plane," remembers Jodie. "When we soared high in the sky, she got so excited. She flapped her wings and I had to hold her down – I wondered if she felt like she was actually flying. Everyone she met adored her. Nobody could believe that a turkey could be so well behaved!"

Sadly, three days before Thanksgiving 2017, Easter passed away from congestive heart failure, a common cause of death in turkeys. Her heart was too big and, despite taking medicine, nothing could save her. She had been ill for nine months with severe breathlessness and on the morning that she died, Jodie knew it was the end.

"I called the vet because she was really struggling to breathe," says Jodie. "And I just knew that it was time, no matter how hard it was going to be. She couldn't go out for walks any more so her quality of life was diminished significantly. She was barely sleeping because of the fluid build-up in her abdomen, which caused her pain. She was so uncomfortable, and I hated to see my girl suffering – I realized I was being selfish keeping her alive with medication. Our last day was spent together making videos and snuggling. I told her how much I loved her many times, although she already knew that, of course. It was a beautiful last day together and I thanked her for always being there for me. The next day, she lay with her head on a cushion in my lap and I stroked her gently until I heard her last breath. It was peaceful, just the way she had lived her life. I felt immediate relief that she was no longer suffering."

Losing Easter was incredibly tough, but Jodie knew that she had to keep herself together to honour her pet's memory – she couldn't crumble, because Easter would have wanted her to thrive, knowing that she had finally got her life together after her divorce.

Today, Jodie has her own home and is studying at university. Whenever she feels anxious or worried, she thinks about Easter and the memories make her smile. Every so often, particularly when she's thinking about Easter, a tiny white feather will float in her path or onto her arm and she knows that it's Easter telling her that she's never far away.

"I believe Easter is with me always," says Jodie. "Our bond will never go away. Just because she's not here in the physical realm doesn't mean she doesn't play a huge part in my life. She was more than a turkey – she was my kid, my best friend, my confidante, the one I turned to for everything. I doubt my life would have turned out like this if she hadn't have graced it – I've got it together because of her. The day I got accepted on my occupational course was one I will never forget. I opened the email from college and, as I read it, a couple of her fluffy feathers floated to the ground. I don't know if they were stuck in my shirt or what, but I cried because I knew it was her and she was congratulating me on finally seeing through a dream. She was saying that I was now strong enough to carry on without her. I will never forget her. Easter made everything possible. She will forever live in my heart and my mind because she rescued me in so many ways and I know that one day I will see her again."

Chapter 3

CHRISTINE AND MICKEY THE CAT

Christine will always tell you that the love of her life was not a boyfriend but her beloved son Christopher. As a single mother for all of his life, the two were incredibly close and they told each other all their secrets.

In fact, she knew that her handsome son was gay possibly before he did, and when he did come out to her when he was a teenager, she couldn't have loved him any more for being so brave.

"My son was an easy child," recalls Christine. "He rarely cried and he was such a joy to have around. I took on both roles of mom and dad, as most single parents do, but he never wanted for anything. Growing up, I always had a feeling he was gay, but that didn't matter to me. I never asked him, trusting that one day he would tell me when he felt he could. I always let him make his own decisions and I supported him. Christopher was more than a son to me – he became my very best friend in the world, and we loved each other deeply. Being gay didn't matter to me at all – I was proud he had the conviction to become the person he wanted to be."

Christopher, an activist at heart, set up his school's first Gay–Straight Alliance group and Christine encouraged him to bring his friends home so that she could become friends with them, too.

In April 2015, when Christopher was working for a mental-health organization, he met Juan, a banker, and they fell head over heels in love with each other. Right from the start, they knew that they wanted to be together forever. All Christopher ever wanted to do was to have kids and a nice house, and with Juan he saw this pretty, fulfilling picture in his future. They shared the same dreams and goals, and they were an excellent match.

"I liked Juan a lot," says Christine. "He was such a kind and loving young man who adored Christopher. They were always doing something – seeing their friends, partying the night away or staying in watching movies together. They were so in love it was breathtaking to watch."

In the summer of 2016, Christopher and Juan were having the time of their lives. They lived in Orlando, Florida, a city popular for its acceptance of the gay community. Christine saw her son once or twice a month for dinner or a movie and they spoke or texted most days, often just to say hello and to make sure all was okay. They were as close as a mother and son could be, and she was happy knowing that Christopher was settled.

On the weekend of 12 June, Christopher and Juan had spent the day at the theme park SeaWorld, and when they got home they were shattered, so much so that they decided to stay in for the evening and get ready for a pool party they were hosting the next day. They had no intention of going out that night – until one of their best friends, Brandon, called asking for their help. Brandon was meeting up with his ex-boyfriend and wanted moral support, so they agreed to go out. It was to be a fateful decision.

An Uber took them to the Pulse nightclub, one of the city's most popular gay venues, where they met up with Brandon at midnight. Later, Brandon and his ex-partner went to the bathroom to talk and that's when all hell broke loose.

A gunman – later discovered to be a terrorist named Omar Mir Seddique, also known as Omar Mateen – burst into the club with a rifle and a handgun and opened fire. Brandon ran out of a back door to safety but Juan and Christopher were still in the club and it was unclear if they were alive or dead. The fate of so many clubbers was unknown for several hours while police dealt with the volatile situation.

Christine, an insomniac, was awake at 3 a.m. and saw that Brandon had put a notice on his Facebook page saying that there had been a shooting and that his friends were missing. She immediately felt in her heart that something terrible had happened to them.

"I called Brandon and he was panic-stricken," Christine recollects. "Trying to stay calm, I got dressed and drove the hour's journey from my house to Orlando – I don't even remember being in the car. When I got there, a policeman stopped me near the Pulse and I asked him what had happened. 'People got shot up,' he said. 'There were many injuries – people are laid out all over the club.' I met up with Brandon at a gas station and he told me that Christopher and Juan would have been directly in the line of fire because of where they were. I clung to hope and I prayed that they were alive, but deep inside I knew they were gone."

Christine was interviewed by a TV reporter in a street not far from the Pulse, begging in tears for information about her son. She became one of the faces of the tragedy – few could forget seeing her frantically crying for help to find her boy, one of many mothers that night who were desperate for information about their kids.

Sadly, 49 innocent people were shot dead by the gunman that night and more than 50 were injured by gunfire. News of the horrific attack spread globally and it became one of America's worst terrorist attacks on home soil. Tragically, both Christopher and Juan perished. Christine learned that Christopher died in the club and Juan was taken to hospital, where he died from his injuries. It was such a senseless act of gun violence resulting in the loss of so much life.

Christine's whole world collapsed when Christopher died and she knew it would never be the same again. It was as if someone had ripped her heart out and she didn't know how to handle her deep, intense grief.

"I was never what I would call a 'cryer'," says Christine. "I had been a police officer at one time, so I was strong, a little hardened to tragedy and, sadly, also used to death in its many forms. Raising Christopher on my own, I had always been very independent, with a Type A personality – crying was never my thing. I just didn't do it because I thought it was a sign of weakness. But when I lost Christopher, it was a whole different level of pain that I had never experienced and I didn't know if I would come out of it alive; it was so raw and intense, like my heart was literally breaking inside."

Christine shut herself away with her grief. She didn't want to see anyone, let alone talk about what had happened. She struggled to answer the many calls from Christopher's friends every day, saying how sorry they were for her unfathomable loss.

Yet, out of the darkness, came an unlikely companion who helped Christine through her worst days and who gave her the strength she needed to carry on without her beloved son and Juan. It was Mickey, Christine's black and white cat.

In April 2012, Christine's mum Minnie had passed away and, while grieving for her loss, Christine had decided to adopt a cat from the local Polk County shelter to honour Minnie, who was also a huge animal lover.

At the shelter had been twin kittens, a boy and a girl, both black but the female had a little bit of white on her face and chest. Both were adorable. Christine had played with several other kittens that morning, but it had been the twins who had won her affection. Although she had only wanted to get one kitten, the female, Christine hadn't been able to leave a sibling behind, so she'd walked out of the shelter with the pair of them.

She named them Mickey and Minnie, and for a while everything went well with the adoption, until Christine found a stray in her yard on the Fourth of July and took him in. This cat she named Cracker and it became obvious Minnie didn't like him at all because he was invading her space. In fact, Cracker really upset the dynamics of the house and while Mickey didn't care too much, Minnie did not like Cracker. There wasn't a day's peace because they would bicker and sometimes fight, so in desperation Christine gave Minnie to her then boyfriend, who was also looking for a cat. Finally, Minnie settled down there, much preferring to be the one and only cat in the house and therefore not feeling like she had to fight anyone else for attention. It was a match made in heaven and Minnie was eventually happy.

Mickey, however, was the type of cat who went about his own business and who did his own thing all the time. He didn't like being cuddled and he rarely even came near to Christine, preferring to hide out in the house, but she loved his independent spirit. Yet it wasn't until she lost Christopher that she saw what a loyal and loving boy Mickey could be when he wanted – and how he would save her from herself when she needed someone to support her the most.

"I had never really loved like I did when I had Christopher," says Christine. "Being pregnant, having him for his thirty-two years – I taught him how to drive, I was there to wipe away his tears, share his successes. When he died, the physical and emotional pain was so horrific. I would ugly-cry so hard until I would scream and gag, and even then I couldn't stop. I would reel over as if my heart was literally breaking into two pieces. It was so unlike me but I couldn't stop. I could go to the supermarket, see one of his favourite foods and have to leave, a mess of tears. I did not know how I was going to carry on without him. For a long time, I didn't see any light. I had no will to live for a very long while. I didn't care and I couldn't see the sense and the reason in staying alive. I wasn't exactly suicidal, I just couldn't see the point in carrying on and if I'd have died so that I could be reunited with my son, I would have been good with that."

During these times, Mickey, the cat who hated affection of any sort, would gently sit on Christine's lap and force her to pet him, even when she was crying wildly, inconsolable. Mickey would put his head under her hand, which would naturally force Christine to look at him and to pet him. His gentle actions gave her something else to focus on, something she says was very comforting.

"I would be crying hard and then he would edge over to me quietly," recalls Christine. "The very feel of him on my knee and the petting action helped me to calm down, to gather my breath and to look at this beautiful animal on my lap. Not only did he calm me down, but Mickey also reminded me that I had to get back the will to live again. I had three cats to care for – Mickey, Cracker and another stray I'd adopted, Teenie – and they relied on me. Sometimes Mickey would look at me as if to say, 'Mommy, you have got to take care of me – we all need you to be well and safe.' It was during these times that I realized that Mickey and I had more in common than I had thought – both Type A personalities, yet here he was, showing me the unconditional love that I had always felt toward my Christopher, and I needed it so much."

Mickey would never leave Christine until she was calm and no longer distressed, then he would go off again chasing lizards and bugs or to sleep in the sun.

He is now nine years old and the pair's bond is stronger than ever. Christine has thrown her grief into being an outspoken voice on gun control in the US – she believes that if there were tighter gun laws, people wouldn't have access to the type of weapon that killed her son.

"Mickey saved my life," Christine says. "I still have hard times but they are getting fewer, yet when I do, he's always with me, like he instinctively knows when I'm going to need him. I love and adore all of my cats but my rescue Mickey definitely holds a special place in my heart. Even though he is aloof a lot of the time, and acts tough, he has the softest heart and he's shown his affection for me so many times. I am so thankful that I took him in that day – fate definitely knew that I would need him."

Chapter 4

GABY AND MO THE DOG

When Gaby saw the advert on Craigslist asking for a home for the six-month-old female pup, she immediately called and asked to see her.

If no one took in Moselle – a Staffordshire terrier–Dutch shepherd mix – she was going to be taken to a local kill shelter that afternoon. Gaby, a lifelong dog lover, had been looking for a pet for a while and the thought of the sweet baby being given a death sentence tugged at her heart.

Moselle – or Mo for short – had lived with a young family and had her own incredible survival story to tell. When she was six weeks old, she fell into a five-gallon bucket of water. Luckily, she was pulled out quickly and given CPR and that's how she was given the name Moselle, which means "drawn from water".

Sadly, her family wanted rid of her. They had let her get away with so much, such as nipping the kids and eating the baby's leftovers from the plate, that she had developed bad habits through no fault of her own. When her family later tried to reprimand her, Mo didn't understand and she would bark. Thinking that she was getting aggressive, they took her to the shelter. It was an all too familiar situation that dogs can find themselves in with families with young children.

As soon as she saw Gaby in February 2013, Mo ran over to her, licked her hand furiously and barked loudly, as if she were saying, "Please take me! I like you!" Gaby saw this as a sign that she was meant to have her, so she paid the $40 adoption fee and excitedly brought her home to start a new life. From that day on, the two were inseparable.

"Mo was a bit nervous at first when I got her home and she wanted to stay close to me," recalls Gaby. "That was fine by me and I encouraged her – I figured it was good for us both and would help with her settling in. We would sit together on the couch with her head on my leg. She was a big puppy even then and she also loved to sit on my lap, even though she was pretty enormous! I swear she didn't know her own size. I loved to paint her nails all sorts of colours and she would let me do it. I would paint them for Halloween, July Fourth, Christmas – she loved the attention and often was so relaxed she would fall asleep. We just clicked from the start and I was so glad I'd taken her in and saved her life. I felt like I was the lucky one for having her."

As she grew older, Mo became more attached to Gaby, who felt the same. They were the greatest of friends – partners in crime – and Gaby always knew she could rely on her girl for anything. It wasn't until a tragic accident in June 2017 that Gaby really understood the depth of Mo's love for her.

Gaby was at a friend's house party and the host had a new pet – Duke, an American pit bull. He already had a pit bull called Dex, who adored Gaby, so she was excited to meet the new addition. Pit bulls are considered a dangerous breed in many countries, but Gaby had never thought that. She always believed that it was how you treated them that governed how they turned out as pets. That evening, she made a beeline for Duke, who was a huge dog, almost the same size as his adopted brother Dex even though he was only two years old. He let her rub his tummy and give him some love.

Later that night, around 1 a.m., Gaby came out of the bathroom and got ready to leave. Duke ran over to her for one last cuddle to say goodbye and, as she bent down to stroke his head, she saw Dex walking toward her.

"Come and have a cuddle," she said as she waved at Dex to come over while Duke rested his paws on her shoulders for a proper hug. But, as he did so, Dex started running and jumped up at Gaby. His huge jaw implanted itself in her face from her forehead right down to her chin and she could feel that he wasn't going to let her go. It all happened so quickly and there was nothing Gaby could do to avoid it except scream as loud as she could. Startled, Dex let her go but by then the extreme damage had been done.

"Somehow I was still standing," recalls Gaby. "I clutched my face and there was blood everywhere, like a scene out of a horror movie. Dex was circling me but Duke stood beside me as if warning him off. Friends rushed in when they heard my screams and the dogs disappeared. I was shaking so hard but my eyes were blurred with all the blood that was gushing out of an enormous hole in my face where my nose had been. As I put my hands to my face, I felt the gaping wound and I tried not to panic, although it was near impossible not to. I screamed to anyone to find my nose so that it could be put in ice and maybe could be reattached. I didn't even feel pain – I guess it was the adrenalin. All I knew was that I was in a really bad way."

Gaby staggered into the kitchen and almost collapsed as her world nearly went black from the severe blood loss. She thought she might die, but her shocked friends reassured her that she was going to be fine as they waited for the ambulance to arrive.

Her injuries were so severe that she was airlifted to St Vincent's Hospital in Indianapolis for specialist care, where doctors were waiting to take her into theatre for emergency surgery to control the bleeding. She was put in a drug-induced coma to calm her down and to allow her body to start healing.

Two days later, Gaby came round to see her sister Rachel standing over her and she felt thankful to be alive. Sadly, the doctors had devastating news. They couldn't reattach her nose because the blood flow had been so severely compromised, so they had repaired Gaby's face the best they could. She would need further, expert surgeries as she healed.

It took a while for Gaby to grasp the enormity of what had happened to her. For days, her head was swathed in bandages and she had to eat puréed food because some of her teeth were gone and her gums were mangled.

Seven days after the attack, she looked at herself in the mirror and was devastated to see the reflection staring back at her in absolute horror.

"I had always felt pretty," says Gaby. "I was a petite young woman with soft features and I always looked after myself. I exercised well and I used face creams to keep my good complexion. The moment I saw my face, I didn't recognize myself. It was like looking at a monster. I felt so ugly and disfigured with that gaping hole in my face and I just collapsed in floods of tears. In that moment, I wanted to be dead. I couldn't even begin to imagine what my life would be like now. People staring at me all the time, endless surgeries to try to make me look more normal – I thought my life was over and I didn't have the energy to fight for it."

Gaby fell into a depression. Enduring severe pain every day as she had her wounds cleaned to avoid dangerous infections, she thought it would never end. She refused to go out of the house for a long time and she would not have people to visit. She was so afraid of what people would say if she walked down the street. She couldn't ever see a time when she would be beautiful or attractive again, or happy in her own skin. Every day was a challenge, but gradually she grew stronger.

And, somehow, despite the extreme challenges she faced every day, she found the will to live and Gaby credits Mo as the one who managed to bring her back from the brink. The week after Gaby was released from the hospital, sweet Mo had been so happy to see her mom that she accidentally headbutted her. Gaby cried and Mo lay beside her and cried, too. After that, Mo was extra careful when she greeted Gaby. When the bandages came off and there was the gaping wound in the middle of Gaby's face where her nose had been, Mo instinctively knew not to lick her face.

"I was so worried that Mo would be scared when she saw my face," says Gaby. "I mean, I looked so different and I had to keep her away rather than risk infection, but she took it all in her stride. She knew not to kiss my face, something she had always loved to do. She would gently kiss my neck or ear instead and then rest her head under my chin as another way to tell me how much she loved me. Mo saw past the gore and it didn't bother her. To her, I was still Gaby, who she loved – that hadn't changed. I may have looked different but her feelings toward me hadn't altered and I took comfort in that. I secretly prayed that people would feel the same."

As the weeks passed and Gaby grew stronger, it was Mo who finally got her out of the house. Mo loved to run and swim in the creek. Realizing she missed those walks, Gaby took her out. But, despite her love for animals, she had developed a nervousness of big dogs. If she saw one, she would suffer a panic attack and have to go back home. So, at first, they only went short distances, but eventually they were back to their old routine. Gaby's heart might still race if she saw another dog, but with Mo by her side she felt safe and was able to let the moment pass and carry on with their walk.

Mo was Gaby's constant companion. She wouldn't leave her side, not even when Gaby showered or went to the bathroom. It was as if she knew Gaby needed her more than ever and she was determined to be there no matter what. During the quiet evenings when Gaby often felt the most depressed, Mo would sit with her and snuggle on her lap. At night, she would sleep in bed next to her mom and Gaby would wrap her arms around her and pull her in close. When Gaby cried, Mo would lick her tears and pull a funny face to make her laugh, or she would put her head under Gaby's hand to let her know that she was there for her.

"People wondered how I could still have a big dog," remembers Gaby. "Yet it was Mo who gave me something to smile about again. Just feeling her heartbeat next to mine and the feel of her soft fur was the most comforting thing in the world. I would cry – a lot – and she would look at me with those beautiful, twinkling eyes as if to say, 'Mom, it's okay to cry, everything is going to be all right. I will always look after you.' Mo gave me so much love and attention that I never felt truly alone – I always had her for company."

To date, Gaby has had seven reconstructive surgeries and may need more in the future. She decided not to press charges against her friend, and after ten days in quarantine Dex was released back to his owner. She couldn't have him put to sleep because he was "dangerous" – she knew he was a good dog who was probably jealous of the attention she was giving Duke, so he lashed out. Any dog could have done the same and Gaby felt it was wrong to punish him.

Gaby has had months of counselling to help her come to terms with the attack and the changes in her life. Thanks to Mo, who restored her faith in dogs, she now has her dream job of working in an animal-rescue shelter. And, thanks to the work of her brilliant surgeons, she looks and feels amazing and has regained a lot of confidence in herself and her looks. She has also adopted another dog, Bruno, from the shelter and he has become best friends with Mo. Together, they are Gaby's world and she couldn't imagine her life without them. She is certain that it was Mo's love and devotion that ultimately saved her life.

"Mo still needed me to be the human I was before the attack," says Gaby. "I had an obligation to get up every single day to look after her. Without Mo, I might have stayed in bed all day, depressed, but she gave me a purpose. She showed me the unconditional love I gave to her. She definitely made it known that, no matter what I looked like, I was the same person inside and I deserved to be loved. Even when people ignorantly stared at me in the street – and sometimes they still do – I can rise above the hurt knowing that I have Mo and Bruno at home to make me laugh and give me a hug when I need it. I truly believe that, while I rescued Mo, ultimately she was the one who rescued me from myself and I will forever be grateful to her."

Chapter 5

AHNYA AND LUCKY
THE CAT

From an early age, Giselle knew that her daughter Ahnya was special.

Ahnya was born a healthy 6 lb 11 oz in September 2004 and quickly blossomed into a happy child who was advanced for her age. She got up and walked when she was 10 months old, and a month later she spoke her first sentence.

When Ahnya was two, Giselle, a single mother from Capitol Heights, Maryland, noticed that the captions were on the TV when Ahnya watched her shows. Not long after, Ahnya started to read those captions and understand what was being said. One of her favourite shows was about a Chinese girl and Ahnya could speak some of the Chinese words to Giselle, which amazed her mother.

"I used to call her my little weirdo," recalls Giselle. "Her speech was incredible before she was even a year old and when she started reading the captions, I knew that there was something different about my little girl. I never put the captions on the TV – she worked out how to do it. As a special-needs teacher, I knew that something was going on; but being a first-time mom, I didn't want to admit to anything, such as maybe she had a disorder like autism. I knew she had a high IQ and, as any mom would be, I was proud of her and I encouraged her love for books and words."

While Ahnya excelled in her learning, she developed little quirks. She was always a little bit "extra", as Giselle would say. If she was happy, she was over-the-top happy, laughing and jumping around the house. But if she was anxious or sad, she would cry and scream as hard as she could, sometimes for hours. She hated loud noises, such as the sound of ambulance sirens or those on a trip to the shopping mall. Giselle had to walk around with several pacifiers, because if Ahnya dropped one, she would lose her mind and make a massive scene, wherever they were. Sometimes it was hard to calm her down and Giselle was often at her wits' end.

When her little girl was three, Giselle sent Ahnya to nursery and it became apparent that she had few social skills. Her caregivers reported back that, while she was brilliant with her reading and writing, she wouldn't mix with the other kids and she was always packing things into boxes, even when other children were playing with them.

At home, she would move anything that she could in order to stack it into a pattern. Giselle walked into the bathroom one day and found all the shampoos and bottles lined up neatly around the side of the bath. During a visit to a family member, Ahnya stacked a tower of boxes so that, in her mind, they were in order.

"I knew that her behaviours weren't typical of a child her age," says Giselle. "I remember I had to strap her into a stroller even when she was five because she would take off running wherever we were if it was too stimulating, such as if there were a lot of people around us at a shopping mall, which she didn't like. Too many times at the grocery store she would stack the cans on the shelves in an order if she thought they were out of place, so it was easiest just to keep her in a stroller. I remember once, at church, she lined up all the hymn books without being asked. It was almost like she absolutely had to have order."

Giselle recalls the turning point. "It wasn't until a really distressing incident at the swimming pool that I realized that I needed help with her. I had gone to pick her up from her lesson only to be met by a dripping wet swimming instructor and Ahnya. Apparently, she kept jumping into the deep end because she thought she could already swim. When I asked her about it, she didn't know anything was wrong, but she got kicked out of the group because the instructor said that they couldn't guarantee that they could keep her safe if she kept on jumping into the water without anybody with her. I was so upset I took her to the paediatrician."

After being evaluated by several doctors, Ahnya was diagnosed as being on the autism spectrum and she was eventually enrolled in a school for autistic children, where she thrived. But when she turned 11, she started to cough all the time. Doctors said it was probably allergies, but medicines didn't stop her almost constant coughing and she would get into trouble at school for coughing in people's faces.

She started to twitch her hip when she walked. At first it looked like she was just adjusting her coat, but it became clear it really wasn't what she was doing, because she did it all the time. She also started to make a chirping noise, so Giselle took her to the children's hospital, where she was diagnosed with Tourette's syndrome, a disorder of the nervous system involving repetitive movements and/or unwanted speech or sounds.

Thankful for a diagnosis, Giselle and Ahnya have learned to live with the conditions. It's not been an easy road, though, but it's a journey that's been made a lot easier with the help of a very special rescue cat named Lucky.

Ahnya had begged her mom for a cat for years, but Giselle was allergic. In 2016, Ahnya was coping with a lot – her autism, the Tourette's, frequent meltdowns and anxiety issues that, although manageable, could sometimes be debilitating. Giselle knew in her heart that the time was right to find a companion for Ahnya, so she started to scour local rescue shelters for a cat, despite her allergies. One day, she clicked on the website of the Humane Rescue Alliance and saw a white, fluffy cat named Snowball in a local shelter.

When they went to visit the cat, another dark grey and white domestic shorthair caught Giselle's eye. The four-year-old female had been surrendered by her owner, who had moved to another house after his divorce and sadly couldn't take her with him. Giselle held Lucky on her lap and was amazed at how soft she was and how much she reminded her of herself. Lucky was pretty aloof and didn't want too much attention, just like Giselle. It was a tough decision between the two cats, but in the end, with Ahnya's approval, they adopted Lucky, partly because Giselle was drawn to her and because she knew she was the right cat for her family.

Ahnya was the happiest and most excited that Giselle had ever seen her daughter when Lucky came home to live with them. Lucky settled in quickly. And, to Giselle's amazement, she witnessed a remarkable improvement in Ahnya's behaviour and in her anxiety levels just by being around the pretty cat.

"I noticed that when Ahnya's anxiety was high and she was screaming or crying, Lucky would appear from nowhere," says Giselle. "I would say, 'Be careful, don't scare Lucky,' and almost immediately Ahnya would calm right down and snuggle with the cat. I remember we had only had Lucky two weeks when Ahnya had a screaming fit about not being able to find the charger to her tablet. I knew it was a bad one because she was hitting her head with her hand and screaming so loud. It was very distressing to see and none of our usual breathing techniques were working. Lucky came and sat on a side table, then jumped on Ahnya on the couch. Ahnya was screaming the place down and Lucky stood on her back legs and pawed her until she stopped and smiled. Then Lucky put her paw on Ahnya's thigh and that was it, all over. I couldn't believe my eyes! I was amazed at how Lucky was instantly able to bring Ahnya back to me so quickly. It was as if any time Ahnya was in distress, Lucky picked up on her emotions and was there to love and support her during every single screaming fit. A lot of the time Lucky wasn't an overly affectionate cat, preferring to do her own thing, but when Ahnya needed her she was always there. It was like watching a miracle unfolding in front of my eyes."

Lucky is not just Ahnya's cat; she is very much the family cat. One day, Giselle's mom Joslin, who lives with them, called and said that she had fallen down the basement stairs and needed help. Lucky had followed Joslin down and waited with her until help arrived and then, once she knew Joslin was safe, went back to her own business.

Another time, Giselle was asleep in the basement when Lucky woke her up, purring loudly and jumping on her chest. She went back to sleep, so Lucky did it again and this time Giselle heard a loud noise that at first she thought might be Joslin using the bathroom upstairs. As she lay there, Lucky, whose hair was on end, slapped her, making Giselle sit up. When she heard the noise again and Lucky jumped onto her cat tree next to the window, Giselle went over and came face to face with a man who was trying to break in!

"I called the police but by this time the man was long gone," recalls Giselle. "It was a terrifying experience but I know that Lucky saved our lives that night. If she hadn't woken me up and that man had got into the house, who knows what would have happened. She's our hero. Adopting Lucky was the best thing I have ever done for me and Ahnya. I had no idea that cats were so loyal and had such intuition. She has made such a difference to our lives, and we love her dearly. I wouldn't trade her for the world – she is a beautiful soul who is the greatest gift to my family."

And Ahnya feels the same: "Lucky is my family. She comforts me a lot. Nowadays I am a bit clingy with her but she tolerates it. She helps me just by being there. I am very comfortable in her presence and when I look at her, it's like we are in sync, especially when I hold her. When our hearts beat, we are the same. She keeps me calm and she is everything to me."

Chapter 6

FAITH AND MICCO THE DOG

If ever there was a little girl who needed a best friend, it was Faith.

In 2017, at the age of just 45, her dad Dave was diagnosed with motor neuron disease – also known as ALS – and Faith's life, along with that of her older sisters Emily and Molly, changed forever.

Motor neuron disease is a rare, progressive neurodegenerative disease that affects the nerve cells in the brain and the spinal cord. Most people will have heard about it because of the Ice Bucket Challenge that went viral in 2014, which raised awareness of the illness and money for research into it. For sufferers of ALS, the nerve cells that move muscles break down over time, eventually leading to muscle weakness and paralysis. There is no cure for this horrific disease and no effective treatment to slow down its progression. Sadly, most patients live for just three to five years after diagnosis.

Before her dad became ill, Faith spent many happy days with both him and her mother Sharon playing basketball in the street and riding horses, her passion. Dave coached local kids' basketball and soccer despite managing a busy lawn-care firm, and he was the picture of health – until one day he couldn't run as fast as the kids at practice.

"He told me that it was like a disconnect between his brain and his legs," remembers Sharon. "But, at the time, he was working very long hours and was tired, so we put it down to him being physically exhausted, and as it wasn't all the time it really wasn't an issue. But then he started with muscle twitches, and after a barrage of invasive tests he was diagnosed with motor neuron disease. To say it was devastating is an understatement – it completely changed us as a family."

Rather than dwell on the diagnosis, the family decided to make the most of every day and create as many memories as possible – before it was too late. For a long time, Sharon shielded Faith, who was just nine when her dad became sick, but it soon became impossible.

"We all felt she was too young to fully understand," says Sharon. "And we didn't want her worrying, but we were watching his deterioration every day and Faith knew in her heart he wasn't going to get better."

In 2019, after several frightening falls, Dave admitted a defeat of sorts. Rather than try to keep walking, he started using an electric wheelchair, and with it came a sense of independence.

Faith, however, who had always been very sociable, playing outside with the other kids from her neighbourhood and having playdates with her friends from school, became increasingly withdrawn from her life outside her house, much to her family's worry and dismay. Sharon would suggest she go visit her friend, but she would always come up with an excuse as to why she didn't want to. It was often that she was "too tired" or that she "didn't want to see anyone". Eventually, Faith admitted her truth.

"I just want to be around my dad while I can," she said very matter-of-factly. "We don't know how long we have got with him, so I want to make the most of it."

Her words tore her parents' hearts into pieces. "I worried about her all the time," recalls Sharon. "We wanted her to be a child, to enjoy her friends and to be carefree, but this disease ruined a lot of things for her – and nothing we could say would make her change her mind."

As 2019 progressed into autumn, Sharon and Dave became increasingly concerned. Even though Faith still loved going to school, when she came home she was obviously sad, preferring to stay in her room and watch TV. When she came out, she pretended to be happy around her dad, making him laugh and bringing him drinks and brushing his hair, but Sharon sensed a deep-rooted melancholy that they couldn't ignore. Faith's sisters Emily and Molly, who are a number of years older, did their best to talk to her, but she never revealed her true feelings. It was as if she were trying to be strong for everyone when the reality was that she was the one who needed looking after. Sometimes she would come out of her room and had obviously been crying, but wouldn't talk about it. The family knew that they had to do something – before it was too late and they couldn't reach her.

For the previous year, Faith had begged her parents for a dog of her own – but with three other dogs in the house, Sharon had always said no. On top of caring for a sick husband in a wheelchair and working full time as a journalist at home, she thought it would be too much effort. But Molly and Dave hatched a plan that Sharon couldn't say no to.

It was December and Christmas was fast approaching. Faith, as usual, hadn't asked for anything specific as a gift, so the pair thought that a dog would be the best present ever.

"At first I said absolutely not!" says Sharon. "But Faith had really been helping Molly look after her dog Kai and had proved that she could cope with the responsibility, plus Dave felt if she had her own best friend, it might help to lift her sadness by being a welcome distraction. I couldn't argue with them. We also all felt that she deserved her own dog as a reward for her helping her dad all the time. As the other two girls weren't at home so much due to work and university commitments, Faith was the one on hand to help me with his care and she never, ever complained. I only had one condition – that we rescue a dog, not buy one, so while she was at school, we scoured the local Craigslist, newspaper adverts and Facebook Marketplace looking for dogs in need of a home."

Knowing that Faith favoured huskies and German shepherds, the search was narrowed down, but they found very few dogs of those breeds who were available for adoption – until one advert on Craigslist caught Sharon's eye just a few days before Christmas.

"It was a couple from a town forty minutes from us who had one male German shepherd puppy and one female available for adoption," recalls Sharon. "I called the lady and she said that their dogs had had puppies unexpectedly and that they couldn't keep all the animals. She sent me photos of both but I knew that Faith would want the male, so I told her to keep him for us and we would pick him up that evening after Faith got home from school. I was so excited I could barely wait for school to end."

That evening, Dave, Sharon and Faith drove to a gas station to meet the couple and see the six-week-old pup. By the time they got there, it was dark. Originally, Sharon wasn't going to tell Faith about the dog but then couldn't keep the secret.

"We're going to look at a dog?" Faith said, not quite believing her ears. "A dog for me?!"

As they pulled up in the dark at the gas station, they could see a truck with a crate in the back and Sharon secretly prayed that this was all legal and above board – it seemed just a bit weird that the couple had insisted they meet there and not at their house.

Sharon and Faith went over to the couple and, underneath a lamp light, they were presented with the male puppy, who was no bigger than a fairly large teddy bear. He looked like one, too, with fluffy black and tan fur.

As soon as she saw him, Faith held out her hands. "He's the last one," said the man who introduced himself as the lady's husband. "No one wanted this little one – he might be the runt but he's a cute one!"

And cute he was indeed. Sharon just knew that they would be taking him home that night – they couldn't leave him because he was just adorable! Faith walked him over to show Dave in the car and he told Sharon to pay the adoption fee so that they could take the pup home.

The pup sat in Faith's arms in a blanket all the way home and every so often he cried for his mother, sounding like a tiny bird, so Faith held him close to her chest and spoke to him so he wouldn't be too afraid.

"It's okay," Faith whispered as she kept him warm in the cold car. "We're going to have so much fun together, my beautiful boy."

After much discussion, it was decided to name the puppy Micco, which is a Native American word meaning "chief", because, as Faith said, he's a German shepherd and she was convinced he was going to rule the roost one day.

From the start, Faith and Micco were inseparable. Her new dog cried almost the entire first night he slept in Faith's bedroom until she got him out of his crate and snuggled into bed with him. During the school Christmas vacation, they spent every moment together playing in the front yard, practising walking him on his leash and watching TV snuggled together on the couch. Wherever Faith was, Micco just had to be, and it became clear very early on that this pair adored each other and were already the very best of friends.

When Faith returned to school in January, Sharon and Micco would wait for her at the bottom of the driveway, then as Faith got off the school bus and walked up the hill to their house, Micco would bark in delight and run to greet her as fast as his stubby little legs would carry him.

It didn't take too long for the spark to return to Faith. She was determined to train him herself, so she practised every day on the lawn in the front of the house while her parents watched, amazed at how fast the little guy learned the basic instructions and how he followed Faith everywhere.

He was such a cheeky little pup, too, making everyone laugh with his antics. Micco would run so fast around the corners in the house that he would bowl over, then jump right up again and run around some more.

"Micco didn't just make a difference to our Faith, he lifted everyone in the house," says Sharon. "He made it clear he loved everyone in his family with his wet-nosed little kisses, and having a puppy again was such a gift of laughter, love and happiness to us all."

Today, Faith and Micco are far more than best friends – they are soulmates who hate to be apart even for an hour. Since Micco joined the family, Dave's health has sadly declined significantly and it's been tough on everyone to watch, knowing that there is nothing that anyone can do to stop it. But for Faith, at least, having Micco around really brightens every day and gives her something to smile about and care for – even when she's worried about her dad and sad that he's so unwell.

"We couldn't have wished for a better friend for Faith," says Sharon. "He is the calm in her storm, her constant in times of distress. One look into those deep brown eyes of his shows a beautiful soul whose unconditional love for Faith knows no bounds. I've seen her cry into his chest and he just lets her, with his head on her shoulder. He knows when she's hurting and feeling out of sorts and his mission is to make her happy, to raise a smile or a laugh – and he always succeeds. I thank God every day that no one else wanted to adopt Micco. He may have been the last pup standing but he really was the best, most gentle giant of a dog who we couldn't love any more. We dropped lucky with him, for sure, and I do feel that we were meant to have him. Our road ahead is going to be a difficult one with Dave's health, and Faith is dealing with things that no thirteen-year-old should have to deal with, but knowing that she has Micco as her personal support system definitely gives us peace of mind."

And Faith knows what Micco means to her. "Everything," she says. "He follows me around like my shadow so he is always there when I need him. He's a goofball who makes me laugh when I'm feeling sad, and at night, when we snuggle in bed, I feel safe. I miss my 'healthy' dad so much. I miss playing basketball with him and I miss Dad coaching me when I'm horse riding. There's so much I miss about him already, but Micco gives me something to focus on and he helps to take away my sad thoughts. I am so thankful that we found Micco – I couldn't wish for a better friend. He is one of the best things to ever happen to me and I love him more than life."

Chapter 7

LAUREN AND THE GUINEA PIGS CONSTANTINE AND CRYSTAL

Primary school was an ordeal for Lauren.

Every morning when her mum Diane got her out of bed, she hoped that this would be the day her daughter finally accepted that she had to go to school because she didn't have a choice. Most school mornings were spent with Lauren in tears, begging not to go and it was distressing for her and for the rest of the family.

After talking to her teacher, Diane thought it was a form of separation anxiety, but she made her go anyway, praying that she would get used to the routine. But being in the classroom was a miserable ordeal for the quiet, subdued little girl who attended her small village school in the heart of the Derbyshire countryside in England. She couldn't make friends because she didn't like to talk to the other kids. Sometimes they scared her, other times they got on her nerves, and so she learned to be alone because it was easier to do her own thing. Her teachers tried to persuade her to mix and to make friends, but she refused. Tears were common and, as a result, Lauren hated every moment.

Eventually, when she was six, she was diagnosed with autism and was given medicine to help with her symptoms. She longed to be at home with her mum and she couldn't understand why she absolutely had to go to a place she detested so much and where she felt so out of her depth.

"I had no confidence to talk and make friends at school," recalls Lauren. "It was such an ordeal even to get me through the doors – I had no communication skills and my parents were really worried. Looking back, I had classic autism symptoms and I was lucky that I was diagnosed at such a young age after a teacher suspected that my problems ran deeper, and she suggested that I go to the doctor to get tested. My mum was very proactive and she took me right away. As soon as I was diagnosed, my life got better. The medicine I was given helped me enormously and I grew to love school. I made a few friends at last and I did much better with my studies. I actually enjoyed going to school, which was major for me. The autism didn't go away – it just got a bit easier to handle once my parents knew what they had to do."

Lauren's life was relatively uneventful until she suffered a seizure when she was 13 years old. As she had no history of seizures, it was a huge shock and she was diagnosed with a mild form of epilepsy. She was in and out of hospital, which affected her school time, but she bravely learned to live with it, just like she did her autism. Unfortunately, Lauren's health problems were far from over.

Not long after, Lauren also developed horrendous stomach pains that would keep her up all night. Once, they were so severe that she ended up in the hospital for two long days while doctors struggled to find out what the problem was. They diagnosed her with severe irritable bowel syndrome (IBS) and she was told to restrict the kinds of foods she was eating, particularly anything deep-fried or bought from a takeaway restaurant.

Poor Lauren's school time was restricted because of her hospital stays, doctor's appointments and sick days. She became anxious and withdrawn as she fell behind in class and her grades dropped. To make matters worse, when she did make it into school, she was bullied by her peers. Being the quiet girl, she drew the attention of the outgoing girls in her classes who knew she had autism and other health problems. She was an easy target and she didn't defend herself.

"High school was the worst time of my life," says Lauren. "I hated everything about it. I think my autism really kicked in again because of all the stress I was under with my epilepsy and the irritable bowel syndrome. For a while, I was out of school more than I was in, and the mean girls in my class picked up on that. It was mostly verbal abuse and name calling but enough to deplete my already fragile self-confidence.

I wanted to retaliate but I didn't know how and, besides, I was always outnumbered. I was known as the odd girl – and kids, being kids, played on it. I can't remember specifics, only that I would get home from school in tears most afternoons. I've blocked a lot of it out of my mind since because it was too painful to keep remembering. I do recollect a girl once pushed me down the stairs while everyone laughed – it was so humiliating, but I struggled to fight back. I don't even think I told the teacher for fear of something worse happening to me. I felt so alone. I didn't have it in me back then. I hated so much of my life. It was sad that I felt like that when I should have been enjoying my school days, which most people can look back on and say were the best days of their lives."

The daily battles to get Lauren to school began again with a vengeance. She would refuse to get up or get dressed and every morning turned into a battleground, which usually ended in Lauren having a meltdown and bursting into floods of tears or a shouting match with her mum.

Tired of the constant arguments and fighting, Diane and Lauren's dad David were at their wits' end and decided to homeschool Lauren. It wasn't an easy decision, but they felt left with no choice. Homeschooling went better than traditional school, but still Lauren didn't do well in her grades. Her parents thought it might be the adjustment but there was more to it than that. Without any interaction with kids or grown-ups outside the house, Lauren was lonely and her parents knew that they had to do something to make the situation work before it was too late.

One evening, they watched a BBC TV show about how animals can have a healing effect on children with autism. Most kids featured in the documentary had dogs or cats and it was fascinating to watch how the animals helped them. Diane and David wondered if a pet would help Lauren. It would have to be an animal she could look after herself and call her own, that she could form a bond with and that would hopefully help repair the damage the bullies had done to her mental stability.

They weren't ready for a dog, but Diane heard of a lady in the village who was looking for the right family to adopt two guinea pigs called Constantine and Crystal, preferably one with young kids who could give them the attention that they needed. The sweet pair were given away by their previous owner when they got too much for them to look after and, rather than have them put to sleep, as they were young, the lady in the village said she would help to find them a new home.

Lauren immediately took to the cute little guinea pigs, who looked almost identical with their black-and-white furry coats.

"As soon as I saw them, I needed to hold them," she recalls. "I took loads of pictures of them; they were just so adorable. They were also very calm and had no problem with me hugging them and stroking their little heads. I knew I wanted the guinea pigs and we took them home. I couldn't wait to show them to my two younger sisters and my brother. I had never had a pet before, let alone an animal that was solely my responsibility, and I felt excited for the first time in a very long time."

From the moment Lauren started to take care of Constantine and Crystal, her mood changed. She would get up early in the morning to feed them before schoolwork and then at lunchtime take them for walks around the garden on adorable little leads that she bought for them. The guinea pigs loved to be walked in their fancy collars, and when they weren't on their leads they played with Lauren in the grass. Sometimes she would let them loose in the house with their toys; other times she would sit and watch TV with them cuddled up together in her lap nibbling on carrots and squeaking in glee.

The guinea pigs kept her busy and their effect on Lauren was astonishing and nothing short of a miracle. She had far fewer meltdowns and temper tantrums. She was definitely a calmer young woman and she was even more focused on her schoolwork, knowing that she had her pets to play with when she finished her studies.

"I was a much happier teenager," says Lauren. "The responsibility was good for me. It felt so good looking after them, knowing they were my special friends. They were my babies and they gave me structure to my life. If I felt anxious and about to have a meltdown, I would get them out of the cage and bury my face in their coats. The feel of their warm fur against my face changed my focus, my breathing would go back to normal and I would be calm again. I would talk to Constantine and Crystal all the time, tell them my feelings and problems, and share any good news that day. They brought me out of myself in a way no human could. They listened to me unconditionally and I loved them with my whole heart in return."

Lauren's grades improved dramatically after Constantine and Crystal came to live with her. With their love and companionship, they gave her a new lease of life away from her health problems.

Lauren is now 18 years old, with a boyfriend, Oscar, and a baby, Valentino, who is the apple of her eye. In addition to being a mum, she attends college in south Derbyshire where she studies travel and tourism. The guinea pigs were given to another lady, a friend, for her children. Lauren says that had Constantine and Crystal not come into her life when they did, she probably wouldn't have made it to college.

"Those two were my best friends for a very long time," she says. "I couldn't have gone through my teenage years without them, much less focused enough to get the grades I needed to get into college. Having the guinea pigs turned my attention away from myself and my health problems. They needed looking after and I took that responsibility seriously. Having something else to think about, rather than how unhappy I was, definitely helped me cope. Who would have thought little guinea pigs could have such an effect on their human? They helped heal my emotional trauma from the bullying and they taught me to be a better, more patient person. I will never forget them. Those beauties showed me what unconditional love is and I hope one day my kids will have their own guinea pigs so that they can find out what a joy they are. I'm so glad we rescued them but, in the end, they helped me far more."

Chapter 8

KIM AND CHARLEY
THE DOG

For ten long years, Kim suffered terribly with her health and her doctors seemed baffled as to what was making her so ill.

Her problems started in 2005 with a random set of symptoms that began with distressing abdominal pains. Her stomach would swell up so much that her waist would increase 10 inches in just a day. The pain was so bad some days that she was crippled by it, curled up in a ball for hours on end, unable to go to her job as a school nurse.

At the same time, Kim felt hopelessly depressed and anxious. She had numerous barium swallow and meal tests to check for problems in her throat, oesophagus, stomach and bowel, but they didn't throw any light on her problems. Doctors performed a colonoscopy, where they examined her large and small bowels with a camera, but again everything was considered to be completely normal, so in desperation she tried to solve the puzzle herself.

"I started on an exclusion diet," says Kim. "I basically lived off chicken and rice for three weeks and then gradually reintroduced the foods I enjoyed or ate a lot of. The idea was to see if my symptoms were worse or better with certain food or drinks. I did find out that I had a gluten allergy but that was about it. That was not enough to account for the pain I would experience at random points."

At the same time, she developed new and disturbing health problems. Her joints became swollen and she suffered with debilitating back and neck pain that even the strongest painkillers couldn't touch. Yet, when she went to see a doctor, he put it down to just normal wear and tear on her body over the years. She tried to live with it, but with each day it was more difficult.

As a chaperone on a school trip to Rome, she couldn't even manage to brush her hair and she knew deep down that something awful was the matter, no matter what the doctors and the barrage of tests said. Things came to a head when, alone at home one day, she choked on a piece of meat.

"I had developed difficulties swallowing," recalls Kim. "I wasn't producing enough saliva and food seemed to stick in my throat – it was the most awful feeling, so I had to be careful to chew my food properly. Then I swallowed a piece of meat and it got stuck in my throat – I couldn't budge it no matter what I did. It was the most frightening experience of my life – I truly thought I was going to die. I couldn't breathe, speak or do anything! Luckily, I managed to make myself sick and out popped that piece of meat. If it hadn't, I'm sure I wouldn't be here today. It was just another awful symptom of an illness that no one could diagnose. I knew that there was something wrong, yet I had no answers. It was frustrating and scary."

Kim was finally referred to a rheumatologist, who suspected that she might have rheumatoid arthritis, but when she developed blurry vision and dry eyes, he knew that there was something more sinister going on.

Finally, in 2015, after ten long and frighteningly painful years, she had her answer – Sjögren's syndrome, a chronic disorder where the immune system attacks its own healthy cells, which affects the glands that produce saliva and tears. It is common to develop it if you also suffer from rheumatoid arthritis, like Kim, and while there is no cure, there are treatments to help, including immunosuppressants – medicines that inhibit or prevent activity in the immune system.

Yet the treatments gave Kim terrifying hallucinations, which continued her anxiety. Three months in, she developed a leaky heart valve caused by her medications and her heart began to swell.

"I was breathless all the time and that made me panicky," Kim remembers. "I couldn't walk up the stairs without stopping, I couldn't go to work and I was signed off for three months. Being at home all the time was hard because I had a deep, morbid fear of death and being alone with my thoughts just wasn't good for me. I developed a fear of going shopping in case I dropped dead and for a long time I was too afraid to do anything. I did go back to work eventually but only part time and even that was difficult."

But being home more did have an advantage – Kim and her husband Clive decided to get a dog to keep her company when she was alone. In March 2016, Kim took her daughter Hannah to the farm next door to see the newborn lambs. While they were there, they met the farmer's Labrador, who had just had a litter of nine puppies. The pair were smitten and bought one of the pups, a fox-red Lab they named Leo. He was a stunning-looking boy with his ginger-coloured fur and he fitted into the family immediately. Having him in the house was such a blessing, as he gave Kim a reason to get more exercise, which in turn helped her rheumatoid arthritis.

Then, one day in 2018, while walking along the canal, Leo got attacked by another dog and it terrified him so much that he was scared to go out on the walks he had always loved so much. It was awful to see the lovely Leo so timid and afraid of his own shadow.

"We decided that maybe another dog might give Leo the confidence to go out and enjoy his walks again," says Kim. "It was such a shame that he was so afraid to go out of the house – I swear he had PTSD or something. I didn't want another big dog like Leo, and it had to be a dog that was agile and liked swimming so that it could keep up with him. I did some research and came across Spaniel Aid UK on Facebook, a rescue charity that places unwanted dogs with new families. I loved the idea of adopting a dog, so we kept our eyes on the page for new adoptions and that's when I saw Charley, and it was love at first sight."

Charley, a working cocker spaniel, came from living in the city with a young family with two small children. From the age of nine months old, she had been chronically lame in her back leg. A vet gave her anti-inflammatory medicines and three months of hydrotherapy, but when the bills got too high and she didn't respond to the treatments, her family decided enough was enough and took her to their vet to be put to sleep. Their excuse for putting their beautiful 14-month-old cocker spaniel down was that she was aggressive and lame. The reality was that they probably couldn't be bothered to care for a dog with a sore leg.

Thankfully, Charley's vet had other ideas. He knew about Spaniel Aid UK and he contacted them for help. The dog was surrendered to the charity, put into foster care and was waiting to find her forever home.

Charley was a popular pup on Facebook and many families submitted adoption applications. Kim got called for an interview with Charley's foster mum and she took Leo along to make sure that they would get on should Kim be chosen to take her home.

As soon as Kim sat on a chair to answer some questions about the type of home life they could offer, Charley sat on her feet and didn't leave her.

"I couldn't stand up because Charley planted herself very firmly on my feet throughout our interview," says Kim. "I didn't try to move her – I thought at least she must like the look of me to do that! I was surprised when her foster mum said that was the first occasion she had ever done that, even to them! Every time I said her name, she would look up at me with her gorgeous, bright eyes and I knew that she wanted us. She already had my heart and I prayed we would beat the odds and get approved."

Out of more than 150 applications, Kim was chosen to adopt Charley and from the moment she went home she was an absolute delight. Kim bought her her own little toy box with her name on it and Charley and Leo played all the time, curing him of any fear he felt while on walks.

Charley quickly clung to Kim, too. Everywhere she walked, Charley's little shadow followed. When Kim was lonely being in the house without the family, Charley was there for a snuggle and a kiss to remind her she was never alone. During the times that Kim felt unwell with her Sjögren's, Charley would kiss her hands and her face as if she knew that her mum wasn't feeling well. For Kim, it was such a comfort to feel her breath close to her skin. Just the simple act of petting her dog made Kim feel instantly better. Work as a nurse was becoming increasingly stressful and difficult as Kim tried to manage her illness, and when she came home after a difficult day Charley was waiting for her – and whatever had caused her stress simply melted away.

In the autumn of 2018, Kim was getting more and more annoyed that everyone thought that Charley was a boy, so she made her pretty floral collars, flower clips and bandanas in girly colours to avoid any confusion. Her creations caught the eyes of her friends who had dogs and it wasn't long before Kim chalked up several orders. Someone then suggested that she should have a stall at the local church hall Christmas sale, where she ended up selling more than 60 per cent of her stock!

"This sent a little light bulb off in my mind," says Kim. "I really did not like my job any more with all the stress it caused me and I had always wanted to work from home. I wondered if this could be a new business for me. My collars and bandanas were really popular and word was getting out, so I spoke with Clive and we decided I should hand in my notice and give it a go. It was a complete leap of faith – crazy really. But all I had to do when I was having second thoughts about leaving work was look at beautiful Charley in her collars that I created, and I knew it was going to work out for me."

And it did work out amazingly. Now Kim works full time from home making collars, bows, collar flowers with pretty centres, and leads. Her business – called Leo, Charley and Me – is doing outstandingly well and she's just introduced a new line of poop bags and matching face masks so owners can coordinate with their dogs. She sells her products, which are all made from recycled cotton materials, tweed and denim, from her back bedroom and is thinking of expanding to meet demand. She has clients in countries all over the world, including Israel, Cyprus and the Far East – not bad for someone who only wanted to make her pooch pretty! Kim regularly attends and sells her products at dog and country shows, where she generates a lot of sales. But perhaps her biggest client to date is UK Prime Minister Boris Johnson's dog Dilyn, known as the "Downing Street Dog".

"Boris would take Dilyn out on the campaign trail with him just before the 2019 election," says Kim. "So I sent him a gift from Leo and Charley – a collar, lead and turquoise bandana with a Christmas print on it. On polling day, Boris was photographed all over the news and on the TV with Dilyn, who was wearing my products! It was such a surreal moment – he was on the front page of all the papers and I knew it was great publicity for my business. Not everyone can say they have an endorsement from a famous dog and it's really all thanks to Charley, who inspired me."

Kim credits much of the good in her life to Charley and Leo. "I think if it hadn't been for both of those dogs, I would probably be a wreck now. They motivate me to get out of bed in the morning because I have to walk them, even when I'm not feeling well. My life has totally changed. I'm more active, I love the outdoors and there is so much less stress in my life. And when I do feel sad or sick, Charley is always there, either on my feet or on the sofa next to me, her warm nose pressed to my skin. We gave Charley a second chance and she gave me a second career I absolutely love. I'm so glad we chose her – there is no way I could function without her. She's a dog in a million who gives constant companionship and love."

Chapter 9

CARLA AND DANIEL THE DUCK

It was love at first sight when Carla first clapped eyes on Daniel, the two-day-old duckling who was being offered as snake food at her local flea market near Milwaukee, Wisconsin.

Carla was visiting with her friend Jim and his wife, and that morning in 2012 the market was busy. People were selling all sorts, from fruit and veggies to cheese, bread and livestock. When Carla spotted the little brown and yellow duckling sitting all by himself in a tiny pen, she had to go to see him – he looked so lonely and in need of a cuddle. As she drew closer, she heard the owner talking to someone else about giving him away as snake bait, and she was horrified.

"I remember he was so cute, just sat there all alone," says Carla. "I fell in love with him. He looked so vulnerable and he had the sweetest little face I'd ever seen. I just wanted to touch his fuzzy feathers! Jim encouraged me to pick him up, which I did, and as soon as I held him in my hands and he was up close, I knew I had to have him, even though I had no idea how to look after a duck. The thought of him going for snake food also made me feel sick, so I literally begged his owner to let me have him. I promised him a good home and to my amazement he said yes, I could take him as he was the last one left and he wanted to go home. So there I was, with this gorgeous duckling, not knowing what I was going to do with him, but I was happy knowing I'd saved him from being a meal ticket."

Carla, who lived with her now ex-husband Matt, took him home and named him Daniel. She read online about how to care for ducks and the pair became virtually inseparable. At the time, Carla and Matt, who had been married for 16 years, were having relationship difficulties and when she brought Daniel home, he took them to a whole different level.

"My husband preferred going out at night with his friends to being home with me," says Carla. "It was a horrible situation – maybe that's why I was so drawn to Daniel. I needed more love in my life and I needed a companion because I was so lonely. As soon as Daniel came through the door, Matt made it clear that he didn't like the idea of taking him in. He hated having a duck in the house, saying it was ridiculous and that ducks lived outside. We argued a lot. It only made me more determined to keep my special little boy."

Carla's maternal instinct certainly kicked in and Daniel was the perfect "child". She bought a baby carrier so that she could take him wherever she went and whenever they were in the house he would follow her everywhere, cheeping loudly with excitement. At night, they would sit together in the living room and watch TV or they would snuggle up in bed together, much to Matt's irritation. Daniel had a squeaky toy that drove Matt crazy, but Carla would never throw it away because it was his favourite.

Matt refused to babysit Daniel when Carla went to her day job – he couldn't stand the never-ending cheeping as Daniel cried because he missed Carla so much – so she took him with her.

Luckily, her job was riding horses and giving carriage rides in the city, so it was relatively easy to bring Daniel with her. The barn where she worked was shared with the local Milwaukee Police Mounted Patrol Unit. Carla took Daniel in his carrier and the police officers would look after him for a few hours. Daniel enjoyed his time with the police, who made such a fuss of him and loved his quirkiness. To this day he gets excited when he sees an officer in uniform.

So long as Carla and Daniel were together, he was a happy duckling who blossomed quickly into a beautiful drake. As relations with Matt became more strained, which would end ultimately in their divorce, Carla seemed better able to cope thanks to the help of Daniel. He wasn't just company when she was alone, he was also the one she talked to and he, in turn, would show her affection like she'd never felt before.

At around 8.30 p.m. on a cold February evening in 2013, Carla was driving her horse and carriage back to the barn after taking tourists around Milwaukee. They were about to drive over a metal drawbridge when suddenly a car ploughed into the carriage from behind. There was no warning and the sheer force sent her horse Nick, who was 2,000 lb, flying across the bridge on his bottom. The carriage was also flung into the air and landed on the road in pieces. The frame was completely bent up and Carla was catapulted onto the cold, hard road, still conscious but in a lot of pain.

The woman driver got out of her car and covered Carla with a blanket and anything else she could find from her vehicle that was warm. Luckily, there was a doctor walking down the street at the time who saw the accident happen and also came over to help. He called for the emergency services and he made sure that Carla was stabilized as the lady held her head in her lap and talked to her. Unfortunately, the doctor was never found again – he disappeared when the emergency services arrived and Carla never got to thank him.

"I remember hearing this loud bang and then we were thrown into the air," recalls Carla. "It was truly terrifying, but I was more afraid for Nick than for me. He's a big horse, but I was so worried he might have been badly hurt. It was incredibly cold that evening, too. My teeth were chattering hard as I tried to speak – I tried to move but I was in so much pain all over my body – I felt like I'd been run over by a bus and I wondered if I was going to survive."

When the paramedics arrived, Carla screamed at them to move her and get to the hospital. They thought that she had broken bones all over her body because of the intense pain

CARLA AND DANIEL THE DUCK **83**

she felt everywhere and, judging by the look of her, they thought that her left arm and right leg were surely shattered.

At Mount Sinai Hospital, around 10 minutes from the scene of the accident, Carla was found to have severe whiplash, a nasty concussion and injuries to her left knee and elbow, and the muscles in her right leg were horribly damaged. As she was being treated in the emergency room, her first thoughts were for Nick. She kept asking if he was okay and repeating herself, which is how the doctors were alerted to her brain injury.

"I was so traumatized. I needed to know about Nick and I wanted to go home," says Carla. "The doctors were very nice but of course they didn't know, so they kept me calm and promised to find out. Thankfully, I was allowed home but, looking back, they should have kept me in. I was later found to be suffering from a traumatic brain injury that was likened to the kind of damage a baby suffers when badly shaken. When the accident happened, the force of the crash into the back of the horse carriage threw me like a rag doll and caused damage to my brain, far more severe than the concussion."

Carla's recovery was intense. She had physiotherapy four days a week for four months. Her left leg and arm had a lot of atrophy because she couldn't use them properly for the longest time. It was, as her doctors said, because her brain had "forgotten" how to use them. It was incredibly frustrating. Carla would tell herself to move her limbs but her brain didn't pass on the order and she became very weak, worried that this would be her new normal if she didn't get better quickly.

She also suffered from debilitating panic attacks and was diagnosed with post-traumatic stress disorder. As a result, she slept a lot, she stayed at home because she was scared of going out, particularly in the car, and she became withdrawn from her friends and family.

The day she came home after the accident, Daniel was on hand to look after her as if he somehow knew that she was going through a devastating time and needed his comfort. Usually, Daniel loved to play with his toys and he would always ask Carla – usually either by flapping his wings or quacking loudly, a noise that infuriated her husband – that he wanted to go and play outside in the garden. But rather than ask to play with his mum, he favoured sitting on her knee instead, snuggling up close to her stomach when he could. When she had a panic attack, or would cry uncontrollably, he would sit or lie down on her chest until it subsided. Carla's panic attacks sometimes came out of nowhere and were very distressing, but when Daniel moved closer to her, his touch was often enough to slow her breathing and bring her back from her own terrifying thoughts. Once, she was outside with Daniel and, hearing emergency services sirens close by, completely lost it, bursting out crying and running into the house, where Daniel comforted her.

Not long after, she was in the house when she heard the sirens again. He pre-empted her reaction and raced over to snuggle up close while she sat by his playpen with her fingers over her ears. The clever duck knew what the noise meant for Carla and he was ready.

"Daniel was very good at pulling me out of those horrible, ugly moments," says Carla. "Sometimes I would cry, sweat through my clothes in two minutes, shake like a jelly, and if it wasn't for Daniel I don't know what I might have done. His presence was a comfort. He even started to predict when I was going to have a panic attack by quacking loudly and jumping on me. When I realized that he was trying to warn me, I was able to breathe deeper and tell myself it was going to be okay, so long as he was with me. Daniel was the difference between me making it through, or not. It was that simple and I came to rely on him from the moment I woke up to the time I went to bed every day."

Four times, Carla held a gun to her head and contemplated suicide and each time Daniel climbed her legs, making the most excruciating noise, loud enough for her to take note and stop what she was about to do. She often wouldn't even remember picking up her gun with the intention to hurt herself. It was like another part of her brain was taking control in those moments, and when Daniel made a noise it shocked her out of the dark place that she had entered.

"I'm not proud that I thought about suicide, but sometimes my life was a living hell," says Carla. "I couldn't see the light and if Daniel hadn't been there I think I would have gone through with it. But he would literally bring me to my senses. I would look at him and think what the heck would happen to him if I wasn't around. It was enough of a shock for me to realize that suicide was not the answer to my problems. He was my saviour. I still don't know how Daniel knew that the gun was a dangerous thing and he had to stop me from using it – I guess he just had a feeling; he's such a smart boy. Eventually I got rid of all my guns because I realized that I wasn't safe if they were in the house."

The only way that Carla could eventually get into her car to attend her many doctors' appointments was if Daniel went with her. She would put his harness on and say, "Daniel, get in the car," and he would get super excited, waddle out of the door and hop into the car. Carla's doctors were at first apprehensive when she showed up with a duck. Many were used to patients arriving with service dogs, but never a duck, yet when they saw the bond between the two they were astonished and realized he was a key part of her recovery. Daniel would obey Carla when she told him to sit in his chair and be quiet while she talked to her doctors and one said he thought the duck may even have the IQ of a three-year-old toddler because he understood so much. Daniel was a novelty because no one, before they met him, knew that a duck could be so capable of understanding and obeying basic human commands. Yet there he was, such a well-behaved boy who did everything Carla asked him to do, and people loved to watch his antics.

One of the worst things for Carla is travelling and, in October 2016, she offered to visit with a family friend in North Carolina who had sadly lost a loved one. The journey entailed two plane rides from Milwaukee to Charlotte and from Charlotte to Asheville. The thought of being away from home and on a plane terrified Carla and she knew the only way that she could get to North Carolina would be if Daniel was by her side. Some airlines do allow people to take service dogs on board, but a duck? Probably not, she thought, but she decided to enquire anyway.

"I called the airline and I told them about my situation," recalls Carla. "I explained about the fear of flying and my PTSD. They actually understood and they said I could take Daniel on board with me if I could promise he would be well behaved. So I put him in a Captain America diaper and we went to North Carolina. I couldn't have him in a carrier – with my balance issues I couldn't safely carry one – so I walked him through the airport and onto the plane on his leash. You can imagine all the stares we got – Daniel was like a celebrity as he marched super-confidently onto the plane. I remember the guy we sat next to was actually thrilled to have a duck next to him – he was awestruck and not worried at all. Daniel didn't try to steal his lunch – I told him to use his indoor voice and he sat quietly on my lap the entire time, looking out of the window or at the air hostess when she walked by. He acted like a gentleman for the whole of the journey and I was so proud of him. You would never have known he was there; he was such a good little duck!"

The man they were sitting next to, Barnaby, was so in awe of Carla's travelling companion that he took a picture of Daniel and put it on his Twitter page. Suddenly, the story of Daniel went viral and every news station in America wanted to know about him. Since then, America's most famous drake has not only helped Carla, he's also spread his love and made a difference to the lives of complete strangers.

Once, Daniel and Carla were in the doctor's office when a lady and her family reached out to say hello. The lady had obviously received some bad news and was upset, and Daniel kept on hugging her as if he knew – she soon was smiling again.

These days Carla takes in special-needs ducks, too, and Daniel loves to help. One, a double amputee, almost drowned in the bath when Carla turned her back for just a minute – if it hadn't been for Daniel shouting for help, he might not be here today. He also tells Carla when the ducks need food or water, or if any of them are in trouble. Normal drake behaviour is to fight other ducks and keep the food to themselves, but Daniel is the complete opposite of how his breed behaves in the wild.

Now, although Carla has recovered significantly, she still suffers from PTSD, which means every day is a challenge, but with Daniel, who is now eight years old, by her side, she is managing to live a (fairly) normal life again.

"Daniel is much more than a duck; he's my lifeline," says Carla. "My doctors registered him as an emotional-support animal to make it official because he is just such an incredible duck. Rather than me ask him for help, he offers it anyway because he intuitively knows when I need assistance and that's the definition of an emotional-support animal. I love him like a child and I couldn't be without him. He gives me more love and affection than any human has ever given me, and I adore him for that. I always tell people, 'Be like Daniel – be a good person!' He loves everyone – he doesn't care who they are – he is accepting in every way and he is nice for no reason whatsoever. Everyone can learn something good from Daniel! He has taught me to be a better human being, that's for sure, and there's no doubt that he definitely rescued me. I'm beyond grateful to have him in my life."

Chapter 10

TAYLOR AND DUKE THE DOG

When Taylor first saw Mike's Facebook profile picture, she had only one thought: "He's hot!" His photograph was of him playing his guitar in a band and to impressionable 15-year-old Taylor, he was the bee's knees. Her parents Deb and Chris saw right through him, though. It wasn't the face piercings and the tattoos that they didn't like; it was the way he played truant from school whenever he wanted to and the fact that he didn't graduate. Taylor was addicted to the bad boy and no one could tell her any different, not even when Mike slapped her across the face one night when they were at a friend's house after she said she wanted to leave. Shocked and embarrassed, Taylor apologized for making Mike angry.

"I should have dumped him there and then, but I was fifteen, I thought I was in love and I had no clue what a healthy relationship looked like, so I did nothing," says Taylor. "I didn't realize what a bad situation I was in.

The physical, verbal and emotional abuse continued, not every day but enough to make my life a misery and force me to walk on eggshells when I was with him. He would call me names and isolate me from my family and friends, but I sort of learned to live with it because he made me believe there would never be anyone else who would want to love me."

In 2013, after years of saving for a place of their own, they moved into their first home and Taylor hoped it would be a new start and a chance for their relationship to improve. A year later, in July 2014, they were married in the backyard of their house, surrounded by family and friends. Sadly, the day wasn't a happy one for the beautiful bride, who felt that she shouldn't be getting married to Mike. The thought of many more years with him and the abuse was horrifying, but when Taylor's dad, who by now believed the nice-guy act Mike put on for them, told her that it was all just pre-wedding jitters, she went ahead and said to herself that things would get better.

It turns out she had made the biggest mistake of her life. As soon as that ring was on her finger, things got worse and Mike treated Taylor as if he genuinely owned her. Taylor kept the abuse to herself, not even telling her parents. But she did confide in her best friend, Thad Gayman, who would listen for hours and urge her to leave Mike and start a happier life.

Events came to a head when Mike started to abuse Taylor's dogs Zephyr, Tahoe and Eevee. He once beat Eevee with a belt and he would throw things at the others, causing them to cower in terror.

"I called Thad and he said he would help me to find somewhere else to live," says Taylor. "He also persuaded me to tell my parents. My mom cried when I told her because she had no idea. I was good at keeping my secret. So I left Mike and moved into my friend Brittney's house. Mike went berserk – he would call or text me sometimes six hundred times in an hour, begging me to go back to him, saying he would change, all things that he had said to me before. I was firm but I swear he was following me, because he would show up at places I was seeing friends or he would just eerily know exactly where I was. But I thought he didn't know where Brittney lived so I was safe."

In the early hours of 17 May 2015, Taylor's world came crashing down around her.

She and Thad were sharing a bedroom, each in a single bed, when she woke up to find Mike hovering over her with a gun in his hand. He had broken into the house. Terrified, she begged Mike to talk to her as Thad woke and implored him to calm down, to which Mike replied, "Thad, you should call your mom, because it will be the last time you speak to her!"

Mike then looked at Taylor and said, "If I can't have you, no one can!" before he pulled the trigger. Taylor had her right hand up in the air to protect her face and the bullet went through her index finger, ricocheted off the wall and then into the back of her head.

As she fell to the floor, she heard two more gunshots. Tragically, she heard Thad gurgling on blood beside her as he lay dying. Mike had shot Thad and then the coward had killed himself. As the paramedics burst into the room, Taylor managed to mouth "Help me" before blacking out.

A week later she woke up in the ICU at her local hospital. Initially, she couldn't move or do anything because there was a breathing tube down her throat. She was told that the surgeon decided that it was too risky to remove the bullet from her head, so it had to stay embedded in her skull. Taylor then remembered what had happened. When she whispered to ask if Thad was okay, her mom broke the news that he had died and she collapsed into her mother's arms in tears.

After a two-week stay in the hospital, Taylor went into rehab, where she had to learn to walk, talk normally and feed herself again. Due to the traumatic brain injury, her right side was very weak but as soon as she could walk a step, she was released into her mom's care.

"I was so determined to walk," says Taylor. "I vividly remember being the youngest person in rehab and the feeling that I just didn't belong in there – it spurred me on to get my life back. I knew I had a second chance and I was going to take it, but it was a long process. Thad's parents and friends blamed me for his death and they still do. I couldn't go out of the house for fear of seeing them or any of Mike's family and friends. It took me a very long time to realize that none of what had happened was my fault – it was all on Mike. He killed Thad, not me. I had to find the strength to carry on from somewhere – I owed it to Thad."

In February 2017, Taylor met a guy called Garrett through mutual friends. She definitely wasn't looking for a relationship but their friendship blossomed and, after six months, it turned into something much deeper. When they first got to know each other, Taylor was suffering from severe short- and long-term memory loss, agoraphobia and horrific nightmares, and it was Garrett who persuaded Taylor to see a therapist to tackle her severe PTSD.

By the following autumn, their relationship had become serious and they moved in with Garrett's father Bud in Philadelphia while Taylor continued to struggle to get her medical issues under control. She missed her dogs greatly, but in the aftermath of what had happened she had not been well enough to care for them, so when in spring 2019 Garrett suggested they get another dog for company and to give her something to focus on, she started to look in the local shelters for a suitable match.

There were so many poor souls who needed homes, but Taylor had her heart set on a golden retriever pup or a German shepherd that she could train to be her service dog for the rare times she left the house.

One day, a friend of Taylor's sent her a photograph of a German shepherd called Duke. He had been moved from a North Carolina charity to one in New Jersey called Compass Rose Rescue and was looking for a new forever home. Duke had been an outside dog who lived with his sisters on a ranch. After they killed a goat – the owner didn't know which dog did it – they were all surrendered to the animal pound and Duke was incredibly nervous there. As soon as Taylor saw the picture, she wanted to meet Duke.

"The first photo I saw of Duke was of a terrified dog with his ears pinned right back while in his cage at the shelter," recalls Taylor. "Far from being put off, I wanted him right away. I looked into those brown eyes of his and I could see so much more than an abandoned dog. I could see a poor boy who wanted someone to give him a chance, to love him and treat him well, like he deserved. We made an appointment so that Garrett and I could see him as soon as possible. I counted down the days because I was sure that this was the one."

Duke was in pretty bad shape when they met him. Deanna, the lady from Compass Rose Rescue, agreed to bring him to the house of a mutual friend who worked with police dogs to see how he did in another strange environment. Duke was very underweight, he had chewed all of one side of his body because of flies, so he was scabby, and his coat was incredibly dull. He went to the corner of the garage and, overwhelmed, sat with his ears back the entire time – it was heartbreaking to see and Taylor was desperate to help him. Slowly, she made her way toward him and, although he backed away, he let her stroke him. Still, she wondered if he would be a suitable service dog, being so timid, but Garrett thought he would.

They agreed to take him home to see how he worked out, so that evening they returned to the house with Duke, unsure as to how he was going to settle in. It was clear that he had a problem with men and Taylor wondered if he had been abused at some point during his young life. He did not take to Garrett's dad to begin with. He refused to go near him and would cower if Bud so much as looked at him, so Taylor concluded that Duke had probably been abused by a big man with facial hair, just like Bud.

Over the days that followed, Taylor was increasingly aware of how alike she and Duke were.

"He was very jumpy, like me," remembers Taylor. "If he heard a loud noise, he would jump a mile and cower. I was the same if I heard an emergency vehicle's sirens or anything that sounded like a gunshot, like a car backfiring. We both also had trust issues. I was still very wary of meeting new people, which was all part of the brain injury, and even when I did, I didn't always like it. Duke did not warm to anyone – it took him months to be comfortable even with Garrett. Even though I knew he would be a challenge, the more time we spent together the more I knew that we were supposed to find each other. I had no doubts that somehow we would help each other deal with our issues. It would just take time and patience."

For the first few months of his new life with Taylor and Garrett, Duke barely barked. If he did, he would run away and hide as if he feared he was going to get beaten. It took weeks for him to feel comfortable enough to play with the toys that Taylor bought for him and when anyone put out their hand to pet him, he would lower his head as if in shame.

Before she got Duke, Taylor rarely went out of the house unless it was for doctors' appointments. She couldn't face going out of her safe zone unless she was with Garrett for support. When they got Duke, she started to walk him.

It was just a little bit at first until she felt comfortable enough to take him on longer walks. Duke was afraid initially, too. If the leaves rustled, he jumped. Whenever other dogs approached, it was scary for both Duke and Taylor: Duke because he was so nervous around other people and dogs, and Taylor because she was also wary of people. But together they were a team that could face the world. They gave each other the confidence to meet other dogs and people, and new friendships were made. If it hadn't been for Duke, Taylor probably would never have gone out of the house on her own.

In the summer of 2019, the pair enrolled in service-dog training and every month they had two private and one group lesson to work on their new skills. Duke passed phase one with flying colours. Sadly, Taylor found out that he had heartworm when they started phase two of his training. Heartworm is a serious and potentially fatal condition in dogs caused by a parasitic worm that provokes severe lung disease and heart failure. Taylor halted his training to concentrate on getting Duke better. Happily, he's much healthier now. Together, they still go out on their walks and play in the garden. So long as they are together, they are just fine.

Duke has developed into a dog who is very faithful to Taylor. He has gained so much confidence just by being with her so much and feeling her love for him. And whenever Taylor needs him, he is right by her side – he senses when she is sad – and is completely in tune with her emotions.

"I am terrified of going out," says Taylor "I sometimes get panic attacks and feel dizzy but if I have Duke by my side,

I feel safe because he never leaves me. He's such a loyal dog. I never used to be able to go in restaurants but with him I can eat out and enjoy dates with Garrett. A lot of people speak to me when they see Duke – he is such a handsome dog and a talking point when we go out for walks. I've made so many new friends because of him and I know if I didn't have him they would never have happened."

It's not just when the pair are out that Duke protects Taylor. At home, if she has a panic attack or a crying fit, he's always there with a friendly wag of his tail to comfort her and to lick away her tears. Garrett sometimes works nights with his job and having Duke around is very reassuring for Taylor. Night is one of the worst times for her anxiety since that was when Thad was murdered and, as a result, she doesn't sleep well. Duke sleeps with her when Garrett isn't home and he instinctively knows when Taylor isn't doing well. He sits with her until she falls asleep with her arms around him and even then he won't leave her.

"We couldn't be without each other now," says Taylor. "Duke is my best friend and the one I turn to when I'm having a bad day or an awful few minutes. I like to think that we need each other in so many ways. I am his wingman and he's mine, for sure. We both have issues but together we are a whole and we can take on anything. I am so lucky to have found Duke. I may have rescued him but he's given me back so much love and protection. Our paths were meant to have crossed and I couldn't love him more."

Chapter 11

NINA AND TRACY THE LEMUR

Nina's 33-year marriage to Ian was a lonely, frustrating time in her life.

Her dad was an abusive alcoholic and she decided in her early twenties to marry Ian because she wanted to escape her father and, hopefully, have a better life. Ian seemed to be a pretty regular guy who wanted a family, like Nina did, but as the years rolled by, it became achingly clear that he was a person she only thought she had fallen in love with.

When their kids Ethan and Jason were born, far from being excited and enthusiastic, he showed little interest and Nina was left to raise the boys virtually alone while she held down a high-flying career in insurance.

"Ian spent a lot of his time reading books about history or calculus," says Nina. "This was his idea of pleasure. He liked doing it so much that he wouldn't put the books down, not even for our sons. While I understood that's what he liked to do, it was at the expense of everything else in his home life. He couldn't see that he was missing out on valuable family time with the people he should have loved the most. It was like I was a single parent for the most part. He had little input into the boys' lives and he wasn't interested in anything I liked to do or say, either. Most of the time it was the kids and me – he was like a stranger. As a result, my marriage was lonely and unfulfilling. It was just awful – no love or passion or understanding. I felt that he put his family second best and so I made all the effort with our kids – we became very close and I lived to make their lives better than mine growing up."

Nina stuck it out for the sake of her children. She could mask her sadness and frustration around them so they didn't know how unhappy things were in their family until they turned teenagers. That was when Nina stopped defending their father, as the boys were old enough to see their situation for what it really was and to see the truth that she had shielded them from for so long.

Nina and Ian had marriage counselling at least five times over the years, but it never solved anything – it felt like a lost cause. She was desperately unhappy until they bought a house and a plot of land in a small Florida village. A lifelong animal lover, Nina took in a couple of stray dogs and cats that needed homes, and she was also given some birds. Looking after the unwanted animals and finding homes for them in her spare time was rewarding and took her mind off her marital problems.

Two years later, she was contacted by a lady who had rescued a lemur called Tracy from a breeder. Sadly, she couldn't keep her any more because a medical diagnosis had forced her to re-evaluate what she wanted to do with what life she had left. The woman had decided to travel the world and experience different cultures before her health deteriorated, but that meant she couldn't take care of Tracy any longer and no one she knew would take in a primate. In desperation, she contacted Nina as a last resort, but unless Nina, who had no experience of caring for primates, could help her, she was going to put the sweet lemur to sleep.

"I loved taking in the dogs, cats and birds," says Nina. "They were easy to look after and I had no problems finding them homes once they had been rehabilitated. But a lemur! I knew absolutely nothing about primates. Yet I couldn't stand the thought that she was going to die unless I took her in – it would have been a tragedy of epic proportions for a healthy animal to be put to sleep. After all, it wasn't her fault that her carer couldn't look after her any more. She was the innocent party and she definitely deserved a chance. After a lot of thought, I said yes, and I'm sure everyone thought I was crazy, but it was absolutely the right thing to do. As it turns out, it was one of the best decisions I've ever made in my life and one that I've never regretted."

Tracy was a 30-year-old lemur who had probably been born in the US. In America, some states allow you to have a primate as a pet if you buy a special permit. Lemurs are originally from Madagascar, where they are now on the critically endangered list because they are caught for food. They are just one step away from extinction, which leaves them in a perilous situation. Animal welfare groups across the globe are working to save them, but the task isn't an easy one. People in many countries, including America, buy baby lemurs from traders and breeders because they are so cute and different. The problem is that, when they get older, without the right care, they become strong, aggressive and uncontrollable. Most people don't know how to correct the problems, so they dump their pets or give them away only for the cycle to start again. It's a sad fate that many of these lemurs end up either dead or in sanctuaries.

When Tracy arrived, she coped well with the change. Nina built her a big cage with plenty of space to roam around and in which she could play on her swings. Her previous owner visited two times a week for the first couple of months to help her settle in and her adjustment to her new home went well.

Nina was scared and nervous of Tracy when she first came. Tracy was just so fast when she moved around that it was unnerving for someone who wasn't used to primates. Tracy would jump around the cage like a puppet, swing from the ceiling on her rope toys, and screech so loudly she was deafening. Then there were the teeth and the claws. Lemurs can bite hard if they feel frightened or compromised, and their nails are pretty sharp, too. Not that Tracy ever tried to hurt Nina – she was as gentle and good-natured as could be. There were times when Nina wasn't sure she was doing the right thing, but thankfully the insecurities did get easier. She found a keeper who would help take care of Tracy until she was confident enough to do it on her own.

It took two years for Nina to put her fears aside, and the more time she spent alone with Tracy, the more she realized what an incredible creature she was. For a start, she was very sociable and would sit with Nina, chattering away to herself. She loved to play in her cage with her swings and her toys and there was nothing she liked more than having her fur brushed. Being around Tracy was calming for Nina and the lemur became a listening post for her frustration at her life with Ian. Many times, Nina would confide in Tracy when she and Ian had argued and she could talk, uninterrupted, and release some of her sadness.

Once the Florida Fish and Wildlife Conservation Commission heard that Nina had taken in a lemur, they asked her if she would take in any more. Around two years after she adopted Tracy, Nina opened her doors to more unwanted animals in need of love and another chance.

Chase Animal Rescue and Sanctuary was founded and, before long, Nina was taking in all sorts of abandoned pets, from pigs, deer and lemurs to century-old tortoises, skunks and even raccoons and parrots. She expanded the sanctuary onto their 20 acres of land with the help of her sons and a few loyal volunteers. While she did try to rehome some of the animals in her care, she decided that, for some of the residents, this would be their forever home. It was a lot of work, but it took Nina's mind off what was happening with her relationship and, for the first time in years, she felt fulfilled because of the sanctuary and all who lived there. Tracy and her friends gave new meaning to Nina's life and that in turn helped her to cope with her loveless marriage.

In 2018, Nina and Ian finally split up for good. She had realized that she was wasting her time and, now that the boys were all grown up, she owed it to herself to pursue a meaningful life. A big part of that was her sanctuary work and nothing gave her a greater sense of achievement than the animals. It was still a painful break-up, but necessary, and when it was all over Nina felt alive again. She was still busy with her day job, which helped support the sanctuary financially, and when she wasn't working she was making bonds with the animals. She had never felt more free in her entire life and she hadn't given up on finding true love, so she took the plunge and joined a dating website.

Not sure exactly what she was looking for, she decided to keep her options open and registered for both the male and female websites to see who caught her eye. Nina didn't see any men she fancied, but she did go on one date with a lady. Unfortunately, the spark wasn't there, so she kept looking. The next person she went out with was Donna – and the pair have been together ever since.

Donna fell head over heels in love with Nina and, importantly, she understood that with Nina came the sanctuary. Donna has devoted her time to the animals ever since they met. In February 2020, she proposed in the primate habitat and Nina had no hesitation in agreeing to be her wife. It felt so natural and like it was meant to be. After so many years of feeling unloved and unappreciated, meeting Donna was a dream come true.

"I don't think I ever thought of myself as gay when I was married," says Nina. "And I'm not sure I even think that now but maybe I was in denial for all the years I was with my husband. Being with Donna was so new and exciting and it felt so familiar, like I had been looking for her forever. Nothing has ever felt so right. When I was growing up, I felt under pressure to do the right thing, to find a man and have a family, so that's what I did. Besides, I don't think I could have coped with being gay back then with all the stigma and prejudice that used to exist. When I met Donna, something clicked inside my soul. We were very compatible from the first date and the level of communication between us was unlike anything I ever knew with Ian. It was like a bolt of lightning and I didn't fight my feelings for Donna. She loves the sanctuary as much as me. She understands that the animals are family and she supports everything I stand for. I feel like the luckiest woman alive! I've found true love with Donna, I have my sons and my animals, and I've never felt so fulfilled."

Friends and family have mostly been supportive of Nina's decision but not everyone can understand how she can fall in love with a woman after being with a man for so many years. Nina and her ex don't talk any more. Nina tried to be friends – you can't erase so much history and two kids – but he doesn't have anything to do with her. And that's just fine with Nina, who hasn't got the time to worry about him any more with all of her other commitments. Through all the unhappiness and upheaval in Nina's life, Tracy and the animals have provided all the support she's needed to get through the bad times and look to the future.

Tracy and the other adopted residents of Chase give Nina a purpose and have filled the void when she's been lonely, sad or felt the world was against her. Chase is now a flourishing animal-rescue centre and sanctuary where people can visit to interact with the lemurs, take part in yoga sessions with the primates and spend time learning about conservation in the beautiful countryside they call home. More than 50 people from all walks of life volunteer in different ways and, just like Nina, they can say that, while they are helping the animals, it's the lemurs who are really their saviours.

"We have volunteers battling depression, chronic medical conditions, the recent loss of a spouse," says Nina. "One lady asked if we would let her husband, who was battling severe depression, volunteer as nothing else was working. We said yes, of course, and, according to her, he has turned his life around as a result of volunteering here. There are lots of stories like this – the sanctuary has saved so many human lives it's wonderful to see. Once you join our family you're hooked, and the animals become a welcome distraction from life's problems and irritations. It's fair to say that you can leave your problems at the gate when you volunteer."

As for Tracy, the lemur who started it all, she is getting on in years but continues to thrive and is Nina's best friend.

"Tracy and I are so bonded," says Nina. "I'm really not sure what I will do without her. She has been my constant and she gave me a purpose to turn the difficulties in my life around for the better. There is so much pureness here. We love the animals and they love us. It's that simple. Some come to us emotionally damaged, others have suffered physical problems, but they all get a chance no matter where they come from. I don't expect anything back, but they give me a sense of peace that I can't describe because it is so true and comforting. This is my life's purpose and, while they need us, Chase will be here to love and protect the unwanted."

Chapter 12

GINA AND ALEX THE TIGER

In the summer of 2015, Gina was convinced that she only had months to live.

For ten years, the former nurse, despite having had a great career, had been addicted to cocaine, a dangerous habit she formed after a stressful time at work and home. What had started as her just trying the drug after a friend suggested she use it to ease her mind and help her cope had turned into a $150-a-day habit. Before long, she had lost a job she loved, her home, her family and friends, and mostly lived alone in her car in Tampa, Florida. All she thought about was where her next fix was coming from. It was a deeply unhappy existence.

"Living on the streets addicted to drugs is a pitiful and nasty life to lead," says Gina. "You don't know where your next meal or hit is coming from or how far you are prepared to go to get your drugs. I lived in my car or with people

I thought were friends who were also drug addicts. I did odd jobs like yard work for the guy who gave me my cocaine, so all my money went back to my dealer, who I thought was my best friend. I had no chance of getting ahead. It becomes a vicious cycle of getting up in the morning, having a fix, maybe do some work, then hang out with your only friends who also happen to be hooked on drugs. There's no escape, but I didn't know what to do. I was trapped."

Gina was incredibly lonely, even though she was often surrounded by people. The trouble was, they were the wrong sorts of people, the ones who fed her habit and justified her cocaine use. She had almost no real friends. The people who cared about her from her previous life had sadly long given up on her and she on them as her drug habit had escalated and she had burned too many bridges.

Once the drugs were gone, so were her fellow drug addicts. She became dependent on her dealer, who was the furthest thing from being a friend, but she couldn't see it. All she could see was her next hit and how she was going to get it. Gina would have done anything – and she did – to get her cocaine, because it had such a powerful hold over her.

She got into trouble, the worst being when she spent a whole week in jail after she was arrested for grand theft. Yet while that experience was terrible and not one to be repeated, Gina had such a low opinion of herself that she felt she deserved everything bad that happened to her. A week in jail wasn't enough to curb her habit.

Once, she was badly beaten up and had a gun pointed to her head over a drug deal gone wrong. It was terrifying and Gina thought she was going to die, like so many of the people she hung around with. In desperation, she tried rehab several times but, with no health insurance – in America citizens have to purchase private health insurance – her options were limited to public services.

"I did check into a couple of facilities," says Gina. "I knew my life was a compete mess. Either the drugs were going to kill me or I would get shot by someone. The trouble with publicly funded facilities is that there is never enough money and too many people who need to be helped, so you can only stay there for a week. That is not enough time to get the help required to get off drugs. Cocaine in particular is such an addictive drug. It can make you hyper and give you lots of energy but at the same time it makes you numb to your emotions. It is like a giant anti-depressant that never stops working. I missed my old life terribly. I loved being a paediatric nurse – the kids I worked with touched my heart and it was far more than a job. To me, it was a vocation. I would never have touched cocaine if I'd have known what it can do. I thought it would be a one-off, but with cocaine it's rarely just a one-time fix. Never in a million years did I think I would lose everything, but I did. As the months and years went by and my previous life as a nurse became a distant, hazy memory, the cocaine dulled the deep pain I felt and, I thought, helped me to cope with my losses when, deep down, it was just masking my feelings."

Things finally came to a head for Gina in June 2015. She had lost a couple of the few real friends she had managed to make to overdoses and bad drugs, and she felt that she would be next if she didn't do something about her life. She knew that she was living on borrowed time, but she didn't know what to do – until she saw a TV advertisement. It was a Humane Society advert looking for people to volunteer at their shelters in the county. Gina had kept dogs before and she had felt the unconditional love only a dog can give, so she applied in the hope that the opportunity might spur her to get off the streets.

Gina didn't hear anything, so, disappointed, she looked elsewhere and, while at a friend's house, she saw an advert on a computer for volunteers for the Big Cat Rescue in Tampa. Intrigued, she applied, never thinking she would be accepted – until she received a phone call asking her to go in for an interview.

"That summer was a definite turning point for me," says Gina. "I felt like, in a few months, I would be dead like my friends or in prison. I couldn't see a way out of the self-destructive life I was leading. Every day was the same – a battle of wills – I wanted to leave the drugs behind but I couldn't; I didn't know how to do it, and it was too easy to get hold of them. I knew that something had to change. Some days I wanted someone to pull the trigger, to end it all because I hated everything I had become. I either had to find a way out or accept my sad, sorry life and that my days were numbered. Losing a couple of the closest friends I'd made shook me to my core and for the first time I looked for that way out, not with rehab, as it didn't work, but with animals. I thought if I volunteered with the dogs, they might save me from myself by giving me a good, honest focus. When that didn't work and I was asked into the tiger sanctuary for an interview, I just had a feeling that it was going to work out."

Gina was right. The sanctuary gave her a chance and in July she went for an orientation. For a couple of months, she volunteered in the gift shop while she learned about the other parts of the sanctuary.

In some states in America, it is legal to own a tiger. Big Cat Rescue, which has won several conservation awards, was set up in November 1992 to take in abandoned animals from all kinds of backgrounds. The sanctuary is now home to more than 50 lions, tigers, cougars, leopards, bobcats, lynx and caracals that have been abandoned by their owners, orphaned, retired from performing acts or that have been abused.

From the start, it felt like home to Gina as she learned the ropes and made friends. It seemed that many of the volunteers had a story to tell about their own lives and they had volunteered for many different reasons. She learned enough about all of the resident cats to give tours, which she loved as she spent her shifts with the animals and the general public.

Within a couple of weeks of applying and starting, Gina had gone cold turkey and stopped snorting cocaine. She knew it wasn't an ideal way to do it, but she figured that, since no other way had helped in the past, she had nothing to lose. It was desperately hard on her body and her mind, but she found something at the Big Cat Rescue that she hadn't before – a renewed sense of love and support thanks to the animals and comradery with the other volunteers. For the first time in years, she wasn't going to let the outside world affect what she had in her present.

There was one particular tiger there who caught her eye – Alex. He was born to a big-cat collector in 1996, a lady who was convicted on 73 counts of animal cruelty. Many of her 86 lions, tigers and bears were sold at a bankruptcy auction, while the others were left to die. By the time Big Cat Rescue heard about the case, just three of the remaining tigers had made it out alive – and Alex was one of them.

Every time Gina walked by his cage or stood in front of it to give a tour, he would come to the bars and make a soft "chuffing" sound, which is the noise tigers make when they are happy. Many times, guests would tell Gina how much he must like her because, while she was there, he was transfixed by her and would follow her if she walked alongside his home. Whenever she had the chance, she would sit beside Alex and talk to him and he would rub his beautiful head against the cage, much like a house cat does against a scratching post. It was during these special times that Gina fell in love with the rescued tiger and felt a bond with him, one that she had never experienced with any living being before.

"I would drive around on the golf cart and as soon as Alex caught sight of me, he would come to the side of the cage," recalls Gina. "It was the best feeling in the world, like coming home to a dog who was always pleased to see me. I would sit and tell him how pretty he was, how much I loved and adored him, and he would listen. He would make this little noise, which I was told was his way of telling me he loved me right back. For the first time in years, I could talk about my feelings without the fear of being judged. I knew, no matter what I did or said, he would still love me. I had never felt the joy of unconditional love before Alex. I had been in so much pain for so long but, with Alex, I could release it. Even though I wasn't allowed to touch him, just being so close was enough for me. It was like he could see into my soul. People ask me all the time if I was afraid of him or of any of the other animals. I have never felt afraid of Alex, or any of the other big cats. Yes, they are powerful, but I've seen a different, loving and very deep side to them."

Not long after she came off the drugs, Gina was reunited with her mother Theresa, who, pleased to see that she was making a huge effort, gave her a second chance. Suddenly, everything was falling back into place. Gina lived for her time at the sanctuary, where she could leave her emotional baggage at the door and be a different, new and confident person inside those walls when she was around Alex and the other big cats.

But tragedy was to come. In November 2015, Alex passed away during a routine dental procedure and poor Gina was left heartbroken.

"I spent a week in bed after he passed away," recalls Gina. "It was all so sudden – he had been such a vibrant tiger, full of love and life and then he was gone. His death was a huge loss not only to the sanctuary but also to me, too. My grief was so deep. I had felt such a connection to Alex and then he left me, virtually all alone again. I guess his kidneys had failed due to the anaesthetic, so it was no one's fault, but I couldn't take in the thought of never seeing him again. Yet at the same time, I felt so honoured to have known him and to have our special bond. I knew he wouldn't want me to grieve for him forever and he wouldn't want his death to start a downward spiral for me, so in his honour I picked myself up and started again."

Gina still works at the sanctuary as a junior keeper, where she prepares food, keeps up maintenance and is involved in enrichment projects for the big cats. Her life is so very different from when she first started there five years ago. She is still completely clean of cocaine. She has a little house of her own and has reconciled with more of her friends. She is hoping to get a job as a senior keeper, which means that she will get to work close up with the tigers, jaguars and the bigger cats, an ambition she's had since she met Alex. Every day working at Big Cat Rescue is a chance to be close to the majestic creatures who give so much back to the volunteers.

Gina has even sat in on surgeries. The first one was Max, who was in the veterinary hospital for a routine operation. Gina fulfilled an ambition to touch a tiger and she got his pawprint on a piece of paper as a reminder of her dream come true!

"I can honestly say that the tigers saved me," says Gina. "They gave me the drive to turn my life around and to start living again, not just for myself but also for them, too, because they rely on volunteers like me. There are so many life lessons to be learned in here. Outside those gates, society isn't kind, yet inside nothing is unmanageable – and if the tigers can claw themselves back from terrible situations, then so can anyone. I know that whatever life throws at me, I will be okay so long as I have the big cats."

Chapter 13

HAZEL AND BOB
THE DOG

During her childhood, Hazel had grown up with working dogs who herded the sheep at her family's farm in Scotland. She loved the loyal Border collie breed and when she grew up, got married to Neil, had children and left the farming life behind, she planned to have another dog.

That opportunity came one day in November 2012 when she saw an advertisement in her local newspaper for someone to take in a Border collie named Bob from a farm in Aberdeenshire. Apparently, the dog, who was a year old, was bred to the farmer's own dogs, but unfortunately he wasn't good at his job and therefore he was of no use to them. It was a sad situation, and when Hazel called to enquire, she spoke to the farmer's wife, who told her that unless someone took him they were going to put the young pup to sleep.

"The wife said that she loved the dog and wanted to keep him, but they didn't need another mouth to feed who wasn't pulling his weight around the farm," recalls Hazel. "Like many Border collies who live on farms, he was an outside dog and she said that she didn't have the heart to keep him locked up in a cage all day because he didn't work. She thought it would be cruel as he was used to running free, so if no one took him she was going to have to put him to sleep. As soon as she said that, I didn't care what he was like, I was going to take him. The thought of her putting down a healthy, young dog filled me with horror and I couldn't let it happen."

When Hazel arrived at the farm, the dog was chained up in a shed and he was going crazy, barking furiously and pulling hard to get out of his shackles. It was clear he was untrained and his bark sounded quite aggressive, so Hazel stood quite close to him with her hands behind her back so he could get close enough to sniff her scent. He didn't try to bite but it was apparent he wasn't used to people. Hazel knew that if she took him home he would be a challenge, but she was prepared, she thought, for anything. She reimbursed the farmer £80 for Bob's microchip and inoculations and then bundled him into the car, and that's when Hazel says that they bonded.

"I had a small car and, as he had never been in a vehicle, he was understandably very stressed out about being in a small, moving space," says Hazel. "From the minute we set off for home, he lunged at the windows trying to get out. Then he started digging at the floor to get away – it was sad to see him in such a state. I kept stopping every couple of miles to calm him down because I was afraid he might hurt himself. I would speak to him quietly and stroke his head when he let me. At first, he was a lunatic, but about thirteen miles into the fifty-five-mile journey home he started to relax a little bit and I felt like he was listening to me at last. Bob calmed down and he licked my hand. I was elated because I thought he must know that I was a kind enough, trustworthy person to come so close and he let his guard down a little bit. I honestly feel that we bonded right there and then. Border collies are definitely loyal to one person and I was lucky enough to be his human right from the start."

The initial six weeks with Bob were, as Hazel says, "hellish". First of all, she hadn't told Neil that she was getting a dog, and when she showed up with Bob in tow, he was annoyed because he didn't want a dog. He wasn't working and he thought he would be saddled with Bob while Hazel went to work at the local primary school. Bob hated to hear raised voices and he would get between the pair of them, barking loudly, to protect his new mum. Secondly, no matter what Hazel did, Bob would not pee outside. It was like he was terrified to go out to the toilet and he would pee up cupboards in the kitchen, against the chair legs and in the living room. It was highly frustrating, but Hazel persevered. She thought that he was so used to being able to pee wherever he liked at the farm that he didn't understand that the house was a no-pee zone. He was also stressed at his change in lifestyle. Eventually, there was a breakthrough. Hazel took some sodden paper that she had used to mop up pee and put it in the back garden. Once Bob sniffed his own scent outside, he started to go there and soon mastered the toilet training.

Another major challenge was teaching Bob, who had lived all his life so far running free in fields, to walk on a lead, which he hated with a passion. He would pull as hard as he could to escape. Hazel would turn around and walk him in the opposite direction so, that way, he knew that no matter what, he had to finish the walk before the lead would come off. An avid hiker, she would also take him out for long walks on the hills near their house so that eventually he associated being on the lead with fun times. Soon, her hard work paid off and Bob calmed down enough to enjoy his outings and actually look forward to them. It was a delight to see him excited when it was time to go out. He even won Neil's heart and became the perfect best friend and companion who loved his life and his humans.

Bob saw Hazel through the good times and the bad, particularly when she split up with Neil and she and the two children moved out to live in a rented cottage nine miles down the road from the family home.

In December 2015, not long after their split, Hazel had been under more stress than usual. Christmas was particularly busy at school and, on top of that, there were still disagreements between Hazel and Neil. Sometimes, she took Bob to school with her as she didn't like to leave him alone all day, and on this particular afternoon Hazel had a staff meeting. Everyone adored Bob so there was no problem with him sitting quietly in the staff room while they discussed business.

Suddenly, Hazel was aware that Bob, who was sitting opposite her next to a colleague, was staring at her intently. He did not take his eyes off her and she thought that maybe he needed to go out for a pee. She was just about to stand up to go to get him when he came bounding over to her, leapt in the air and hit her straight in her stomach with his paws.

"When I saw him looking at me, I knew something was wrong," recalls Hazel. "His gaze was so intense but I figured he must just need to go out for a little walk and the toilet. When he hit me in the stomach with his full force, he winded me as I was knocked into the chair. It was so out of character for him to misbehave like that, as normally he was the perfect, quiet dog at school. I eventually took him outside but he still seemed out of sorts, even when we got home later. It was weird and I couldn't put my finger on what was the matter with him."

The next morning, Hazel's stomach had become swollen and tender, so much so that she thought she may have developed a hernia. She booked an appointment with her doctor, a family friend, who asked her if she would be happy for a female doctor to examine her.

The next thing she knew, she was on her way to the hospital for an ultrasound scan of her increasingly swollen stomach and Hazel could tell from the look on the technician's face that something was wrong. It wasn't until after Christmas that a CT scan showed a tumour, 19 cm across, shaped a bit like a rugby ball. It was growing very quickly and was attached to her ovaries. Hazel looked pregnant because her stomach was so swollen with fluid that had to be drained. Yet she had also lost a lot of weight and was just five and a half stone of skin and bone. Doctors later biopsied the growth, which by then was 29 cm in length, but the results came back inconclusive.

As the tumour was growing so quickly and it had attached itself to her bowel, they said that she needed urgent surgery to remove it or she may have to have a colostomy bag for the rest of her life. Her oncologist also warned her that if she didn't have the surgery, she would be dead within six weeks and that she would have a "horrible death" with a lot of pain.

Hazel had been reading about ovarian cancer and she knew that the odds were stacked against her. Most women don't know that they have it until it's too late to treat or cure since symptoms mirror other, less serious illnesses. It's no surprise that ovarian cancer is known as the silent killer, and so mentally Hazel prepared herself for the worst while hoping for the best. All she knew was that she was going to fight the cancer – she had Bob and her two kids to think about.

In February 2016, she tearfully said goodbye to Bob, who stayed with her friend Debbie, and she went to the hospital with her mum and children Rory and Corrie, who came for moral support before her surgery the next day.

It was a mammoth operation lasting ten and a half hours. Three doctors worked on Hazel and they removed her ovaries and performed a full hysterectomy. They were able to rebuild her bowel and remove cancer cells from her diaphragm, liver, spleen and the lining of her abdomen, which was covered in a blister-like substance that caused the excess fluid and swelling. Further tests showed that Hazel definitely had ovarian cancer but it was low grade, which meant that it had grown very slowly until it was disturbed, when it began expanding rapidly. Her doctors estimated she could have had it for at least ten years and had never known, and then for whatever reason the cancer had turned ugly and spread around her body.

Hazel had four sessions of chemotherapy that made her very sick, but she got to keep her hair, and soon she was declared to be in remission, which was hailed a miracle by her doctors. Debbie kept Bob for about a month until Hazel was well enough to leave the cottage and walk him. Their reunion was beautiful.

"I remember I was stood at the door of the cottage with a cushion to protect my stomach, waiting for him to come home," says Hazel. "I had missed my boy so much – I couldn't wait to see him. As soon as he saw me down the path, he ran, jumped up the steps into the cottage, whimpering softly, and then he lay on his back. He was so pleased to see me; I'm sure he had wondered if he would ever do so again. It was a beautiful moment. I had missed him so very much. I needed him more than anything at that time and, without him, I don't think my recovery would have been so quick. He made me feel so loved and cherished."

Bob stayed by her side and was a huge comfort to Hazel. He picked up on her moods and was always there to cheer her up by barking and making goofy faces, or just by lying next to her so she could feel his fur against her skin.

There were good and bad days, but Hazel was determined to get better. After a year, she and Neil got back together, and if it hadn't been for Bob she doesn't know how she would have got through her cancer battle. Bob gave her a reason to get better quickly because she knew he missed his walks in the hills, so little by little, every day, they walked longer distances together until Hazel was back up to full strength. Thankfully, she is still in remission and she credits Bob with saving her life.

"I really believe that he knew I had cancer and that's why he jumped up at me that day to alert me," says Hazel. "I think he could sniff that I was ill – cancer has a very distinct smell to some dogs. When he jumped on my stomach, my muscles hurt and allowed the swelling to come out. I had always been so fit from all of my hiking and I think that's why I didn't get ill quicker. My own body hid the cancer for so long until Bob disturbed it. He saved my life in so many ways. I wouldn't be here if he hadn't detected the cancer. I owe him so much. Bob is my best friend, my everything – he's my world along with my children and Neil. I can't imagine ever replacing him. I realize how fortunate I am to be here. Many women with ovarian cancer don't get as lucky and they don't have a Bob to help with their recoveries. He is my angel, my therapist when the days are tough. He's the one I can laugh and smile with and I am so thankful for our unconditional bond. Bob is simply the best."

Chapter 14

LUANA AND NURSE ZULU THE CAT

In the spring of 2001, Luana noticed that the black and white cat who lived next door was heavily pregnant. The cat, named Yardie, was well known in the street in Leeds, England for being wild and crazy. She would chase the biggest dogs, fight other cats and was horrible to humans. Yardie wouldn't be touched or stroked by anyone and her owner had had enough.

"She's pregnant again!" the neighbour told Luana. "I'm sick of her. I can't be bothered – she's a pain."

Without hesitation, Luana, who loved all animals, offered to have Yardie. The thought of her being alone in a basement having her kittens was heartbreaking. She came up with a story about how she had always wanted to see kittens being born and Yardie's owner was only too pleased to get rid of her.

"Luckily, the owner said yes right away," remembers Luana. "I took her home and for some reason she took to me right away. Maybe it was because I showed her the love, care and attention that she had been lacking. I believe all animals are products of their environments and I didn't like her previous owner. I could see that there was no love lost between them – the lady was loud, and I felt sure that Yardie got horrible vibes from her. Yardie was lovely to me but she hated everyone else. She would chase boxer dogs down the street, hiss and claw at people who walked too close to her, and, if anyone came into my house, she would try to hurt them. At just two years old, she had already had two litters of kittens. I felt sorry for her and changed her name to Mother, as it seemed more fitting. I didn't care that she acted crazy – I was patient and I believed that my love would change her."

Mother had three kittens in June: one all-black little girl called Monkey and two black-and-white kittens that Luana called James and Zulu. They were beautiful and, although she had found homes for them, Luana couldn't let any of them go.

Out of the three babies, it was the girl Zulu who bonded with Luana, whose life at the time was very volatile. At 21 years old, she worked in a nightclub and had fully adopted the party lifestyle. Every night she went home drunk and sometimes her drinking sessions lasted for 72 hours or more. When she became a bartender at the club, her situation got worse. She would sometimes go to work drunk, but, because she was good at her job, she was often reprimanded but never sacked. At the time, it felt like there was no escape from the path that she was on and Luana hated herself. She was confused about what she wanted out of life, she had no self-worth, no confidence, and alcohol became her mask to hide behind.

Most mornings, when Luana was hungover and sick to her stomach, Zulu would sit beside her patiently and wait until she was well enough to get up, although Luana didn't notice her devotion until one morning after a particular bender.

"I woke up on the couch and Zulu was sat on my chest, purring gently," recalls Luana. "I felt panicked because I didn't remember how I got home – I must have blacked out the night before. I had such a dark feeling in the pit of my soul. I had no recollection of the previous night because I had been so drunk. My then boyfriend came downstairs and he said that I had been passed out for twelve hours and that Zulu had not moved from my chest in all that time. That's when I nicknamed her Nurse Zulu because it occurred to me that every time I felt ill or sad – which was all the time, it seemed – she was there next to me. I hated my life. I wasn't where I wanted to be and yet I was stuck in a cycle of heavy drinking and working. I would sit and cry for hours sometimes, ashamed at what I was turning into, but not knowing how to change. The only really good thing in my life was Zulu and I knew that, no matter how I behaved, she would love me anyway. There's a lot to be said for feeling that kind of unconditional affection at a time when I couldn't even love myself."

Luana eventually moved on from the nightclub scene, met a heating engineer called Tom and in 2009 the pair eloped to Jamaica to get married. Later, back home, they had two perfect daughters and Luana felt that she was finally living the way she was meant to live. For the first time in her life, she could say she was truly happy with herself. Tom was a wonderful husband and father and Luana thought they had a strong marriage.

Then, in January 2017, Tom dropped a huge bombshell, which floored Luana because she did not see it coming at all. He broke the news to his wife of seven years that he was transgender and that, after much agonizing thought, he wanted to live as "Kara" and eventually have a sex change.

Over the years, Tom had asked to try on Luana's clothes and she had thought nothing of it. On their wedding day, he had even asked to try on her dress, which seemed an odd request but Luana had said yes to it because she thought it was all a big joke. Never in a million years could she have been prepared for his confession.

Immediately, she felt that their relationship had been built on lies and it was an agonizing time as she struggled to come to terms with effectively losing the husband she adored. But after a lot of soul-searching and tears, she decided that the only way forward was to support Kara, so they signed her up for private hormone treatment and Tom began to live as a woman.

"After a lot of thought and confusion, I was proud that Tom had the courage to live the life he really wanted," says Luana. "I truly believe that everybody has to the right to be themselves, so long as they are not hurting anybody. We explained the changes the best we could to the girls and, honestly, they weren't that bothered – to them he was still their daddy no matter what. He may have had a blonde wig and worn skirts and leggings, but they didn't mind. I was prepared to live with him as Kara until the hormones kicked in, and then I knew I'd feel differently toward her. It's hard to explain but I felt the need that we should both move on with our lives. Although I was still supportive, I couldn't live like 'best friends' and so we split up. It wasn't a terrible decision because we were sensible and amicable, but it still hurt like hell."

Six months later, Kara had another surprise for her family. She told Luana that she wanted to stop all the hormone therapy and go back to being a man. It was the most confusing part of the whole sex-change saga for Luana. Kara's initial, monumental decision to become a woman had ended their marriage, yet now she was reversing the biggest change ever made to any of their lives. Luana couldn't understand what had altered in so short a time. Had six months of living like a woman been worth the fact that it had ended an otherwise loving and happy marriage?

Kara didn't have any answers, either. While she didn't regret her decision to become a woman, she was sure that she didn't want to be Kara any more. She missed being daddy Tom, who had always been a "man's man" who loved football and a pint with his friends in the local pub. Now Tom again, he stopped the therapies and even grew a beard. Luana and Tom remained good friends and, even after Luana met someone new, her current partner Alex, Tom moved to Portugal with them and stayed for a while for the sake of the children.

Throughout the anguish and the turmoil of that year, Nurse Zulu was Luana's best friend, her constant in a deep sea of uncertainty. Whenever she stopped to sit or she went to bed, Nurse Zulu was there, often on her chest, gently pressing her little paws into Luana's body – it was a huge comfort to feel her so close. If Luana broke down and cried, sweet Nurse Zulu would lick away her tears and purr as if she were telling Luana that everything was going to work out. Just her presence was enough sometimes to raise a smile in the knowledge that, no matter how lonely she was, or how unhappy, she always had Nurse Zulu.

In 2019, Luana hit a new low point in her life when she lost more than £40,000 trying to help a friend, both in the woman's private life and by investing in her company. Being the person that she is, Luana had gone above and beyond with the time and effort she'd put into the relationship and the firm, but things did not turn out as she expected, as she found out the state of company had been vastly misrepresented to her. Luana lost the house she was buying and almost her own successful PR business because of it. She sunk into a deep depression. She couldn't see a way forward and she felt a complete failure that she had allowed herself to put so much at risk. Life as she knew it came to a grinding halt and some days her biggest achievement was just getting out of bed and putting one foot in front of the other. Luana had no idea how she was going to claw her way back, but she had help – Nurse Zulu came to her rescue again, once more providing the comfort and care she so badly needed, guiding Luana back to where she needed to be and reinstilling her self-belief.

Luana and Alex had a baby in the summer of 2021 and her business is thriving again. She says that, if it wasn't for Nurse Zulu's love and support, she wouldn't be where she is today.

Nurse Zulu is now more than 20 years old but she's still going strong. Luana had severe morning sickness in the beginnings of her pregnancy and, of course, Nurse Zulu didn't leave her side once. In fact, Luana and Nurse Zulu share a bedroom in their home in Anglesey, Wales. It's been that way ever since the baby was born and, as Alex wasn't keen on a cat sleeping with them, he decided it was probably easiest if he just moved into the spare bedroom!

"Nurse Zulu is incredible," says Luana. "I couldn't have asked for a better cat. I'm so glad I rescued her mum all those years ago or I would never have known her and my life would be so much less without her. She's old now and rarely leaves the bedroom where I've made her a little camp. I have so much to thank her for. Throughout the most awful, difficult times in my life she has been the most faithful and loving companion anyone could ask for. I truly believe that I am her human. I pray she has many more years left in her because I can't imagine being without her. She's my soulmate and I love her more than I could ever say."

Chapter 15

LISETTE AND BEAUTIE THE THREE-LEGGED DOG

Lisette has a long and deep affinity for dogs that started when she was 15 years old when she got Phoebe, her very own Westie. The pair were inseparable for years as they grew up together, never far apart. Phoebe was Lisette's constant companion through the important developments in her life and she loved her much more than as a dog – she was one of the closest friends she ever had.

When Lisette eventually left home to pursue a successful career in marketing, she moved from country to country with her job, so it wasn't possible to have any more pets. Instead, she volunteered at rescue centres wherever she was in the hope that her efforts would make a difference in the lives of unwanted dogs and fulfil her need to have a pup in her life.

In August 2013, Lisette and her husband Dan, a chemistry teacher, moved to Dubai for her job as the head of marketing for a group of healthcare providers, and they lived on the sixteenth floor of a high-rise apartment building. Quickly, she saw that Dubai had a major problem with stray dogs, and it broke her heart.

"When we moved to Dubai, it was clear that there were many dogs who lived on the streets," says Lisette. "Everywhere you looked, they were rummaging for food or running away trying to hide because they were so scared. Very few people stop to help them as they are considered nothing more than a nuisance, a bit like vermin. It's sad but unfortunately that's what it's like over there. I hate to say it, but a big cause of the problem was the large numbers of expats who live there. They get a dog, then when they have to leave a few years down the line they don't take their pets with them because it's expensive to transport an animal back home. I've heard of dogs being thrown out of windows into the streets; others are left in their apartments with little food or water. Only the lucky ones, if you can call them that, end up in the shelters with any chance of being adopted. It was sickening to see, and I desperately wanted to do something to help."

Lisette volunteered for Animal Action, a large charity that takes in unwanted dogs and rehomes them wherever possible. It's a difficult job because there are so many animals that can't be helped, but Lisette needed to work there. She would go out in the evenings to leave food for the dogs who couldn't be caught, drive dogs to their foster homes while they waited to be matched with a family, and helped out on adoption days, which were fun and satisfying when a dog found a forever family.

It was during an adoption day that she first saw Beautie, a pretty rescue thought to be a Saluki (desert dog) crossed with a Border collie. The poor girl was about a year old and had been knocked down by a car while living on the streets. Luckily for her, a passer-by scooped her up and got her help, but she sadly lost a hind leg in the accident. She had been to a couple of foster homes without finding anywhere permanent, but there she was, a three-legged bundle of absolute joy, hoping to find a home that day. Lisette immediately took to her and felt an instant connection with her. She was the happiest dog she had ever seen, despite having only three legs, and she talked to everybody! But as Lisette and Dan lived in a high-rise apartment, she thought there might be more suitable environments to keep a dog and so she worked hard to get other people interested in Beautie.

About a month later, Lisette read a Facebook post about Beautie on the Animal Action page. It was a desperate, last-ditch appeal for a foster for Beautie, as she was living in a crate at a veterinary clinic. Her most recent foster decided she was too much trouble with only having the three legs and had sent her back, so she was alone again.

Seeing her stuck in a crate moved Lisette and she offered to foster the little dog who had captured her heart at the adoption event. Lisette and Dan picked her up that same day and took her home. That evening, on a walk, they met a woman with her own dog who said that she was very interested in taking Beautie. The woman suggested a doggy playdate to see how they got on – but, as she said it, Lisette had second thoughts about letting Beautie go.

"I turned to Dan and I said I didn't like the thought of a playdate to find her a family," recalls Lisette. "I didn't want her going anywhere else and Dan completely agreed – we wanted to adopt her. She had been so good when we had picked her up and brought her home. We realized that being in the apartment didn't matter as much as we thought because there were places to walk outside, and Beautie had really made herself at home. I remember looking at her lovely little face and I knew I couldn't let her go to anyone else – it was that simple. She needed us and, although I didn't know it at the time, we needed her just as much."

A few days later, Lisette got a phone call from Holland, where her parents Denise and John lived. John, who had been ill with a lung disease for several years, had suffered a sudden heart attack and died. His death was unexpected, and it shook Lisette's family to the core. Lisette immediately flew out to Holland and Dan put Beautie into a day care while they were away. They hadn't even adopted her yet, which upset Lisette, who felt guilty she had to leave her.

It would have been all too easy to wallow in grief and stay in Holland indefinitely to support her family but, as her mum Denise pointed out, she had to get back to Dubai for Beautie, who relied on her.

It wasn't easy for Lisette to return to Dubai. She struggled to say goodbye to her mum, and when she did get back she felt so alone at times thinking about her dad and how much he would be missed. It was during these moments that Beautie had a knack of being there for her when she needed it the most, and it didn't matter what time of the day or where they were. She would sit and lick away Lisette's tears or lie in her arms for hours and would always eventually manage to put a smile on her mum's face. Having Beautie also kept Lisette in a routine rather than sitting inside all the time, lounging around doing nothing except thinking about things that made her feel sad. She had to take Beautie out for walks every day – just getting out into the fresh air was good for her mental state. It was during these times that she appreciated Beautie even more.

"I do wonder if it was coincidence or if it was meant to be that we got Beautie right before my dad died," says Lisette. "She guided me through one of the most difficult times in my life. She had an incredible intuition of knowing how I was feeling and then snuggling up to me accordingly – she was, and still is, a huge cuddler. Feeling her breath on my neck was so healing. Sometimes I would cry so hard for my dad that I would make myself feel ill, and Beautie never left my side. I feel that we were meant to have her and she was sent to rescue me from my own grief. I am thankful every day that we decided to take her in."

In 2017, Lisette and Dan moved to a village in West Yorkshire, England. Inspired by Beautie, Lisette began to research the plight of abandoned dogs in the area. Sadly, the situation wasn't that much better than in Dubai. According to research by the Dogs Trust, around 130,000 dogs get abandoned in the UK every year. Given that figure is now from several years ago, the numbers are quite possibly much higher these days, and may have also been impacted by the coronavirus pandemic that ravaged the world. And Lisette's own findings were equally heartbreaking. The reasons why dogs were getting abandoned varied from valid causes, such as the death of their owner, to absurd ones, such as people preferring to spend their money on a holiday but not pay for their dog to be boarded. One of the most upsetting things she discovered was that most of the dog rescue centres were struggling to survive due to the sheer numbers of abandoned dogs.

Lisette longed to help in any way that she could so that many more dogs like her Beautie had the chance of finding real, loving families. She got together with her cousin Lee Brown, who was an entrepreneur and who adored rescue dogs just as much as she did. Together they brainstormed ways to raise money for the rescue centres and to reduce the numbers of homeless dogs. In the summer of 2020, they launched DoggyLottery, a non-profit company that raises valuable funds for dog rescue centres through monthly online lotteries. Every month, five different rescue centres are nominated by the public and partnered with DoggyLottery, which sells tickets for £1.50 each. Most of the proceeds go directly to the charities or rescue centres voted for by the public buying the lottery tickets. The more votes a centre gets, the bigger their share of the charity fund.

To date, more than £11,000 has been donated and the lottery is growing. Lisette, who lost her job due to the Covid-19 pandemic, has devoted herself to running the charity and each week sales are increasing as more people hear about it. With Beautie as the DoggyLottery's official mascot, Lisette is confident that this is their calling and that one day the charity will boom and make a huge difference in the lives of shelter pets.

"My Beautie is my inspiration and motivation to find a way of doing more for rescue dogs," says Lisette. "She may not be human, but she is my baby, and from the time I wake up in the morning she puts a smile on my face. If it hadn't been for her, I'm not sure I would have got over what happened to my dad. She was the best reason in the world to carry on and she watches over me – my guardian, always there if I need her. Beautie also inspires me to lead my best life. When we go out, people stare at her because she is missing a leg and I want to tell them not to focus on the negative because she doesn't – she's happy as she is! She is also a registered pet-therapy dog – we have been into care homes before Covid and the residents absolutely adore her! She is so good with people – I can take her anywhere and she raises a smile. We will continue to count our blessings and fight for other rescue dogs – it is definitely our mission in life, and we will never give up. While she is by my side, I can do anything."

Chapter 16

HANNAH AND BLU THE BUDGIE

When Hannah's best friend Rachel and her family left the neighbourhood and moved almost 3,000 miles away to start a new life, Hannah was understandably devastated. The girls had known each other from being babies living two houses apart in their suburban Florida neighbourhood.

They were both so alike. Sassy, beautiful, long-haired blonde children with a real zest for life – and hot and spicy Cheetos! Every day after school they would go to the other's house to swim or play in the street. They were never bored when they were together, and they couldn't ever imagine not being with the other. Until that one day came and Rachel moved to California when she was ten years old.

In tears, Hannah waved her on her way to the airport and the pair made a vow to call frequently and write and send pictures when they had the chance.

"Those girls were inseparable," recalls Liz, Hannah's mom. "From as soon as they could talk and walk, they were together, and Rachel's mom Sarah and I loved that they were so close. It was like having a second daughter, and although they did play with the other kids in the street, they were happiest when it was just the two of them swimming or riding their bikes in the estate. I liked to think that they would always have each other's backs, even when they were teenagers. So when Sarah told me that they were moving to California, my first thought was for Hannah and how sad she would be. Right up until they moved, I don't think either girl could believe it was happening. Both were incredibly upset and all we could do as mothers was comfort them. It was very sad."

After Rachel moved, something changed in Hannah. She was quieter than she had ever been in her life and she would sit in her room listening to music or watching the television. It was clear that she was lonely. She could have played with the kids down the road, and she sometimes did; but although they were lovely, they weren't Rachel, and she didn't have the same relationship with them.

Liz persuaded Hannah to join a local Girl Scout group to make more friends, which she did, but not having Rachel by her side was hard. They always gave each other the confidence to withstand new situations, and now she was gone. It was a lot to come to terms with.

The girls talked on the phone fairly frequently, but then with the three-hour time difference it was more difficult than they had thought and gradually their communication tapered off as Rachel started a new school and made new friends.

Worried that the spark had gone from Hannah, Liz was unsure what to do. It was obvious her daughter was sad nearly all of the time and she didn't make much effort with her other friends. She wasn't in a good place. At a time when she shouldn't have a care in the world, losing Rachel had really affected her and she was content to be home alone with the family dog Pete for company.

One day at Girl Scouts, one of the dads mentioned that he was looking for a home for his blue budgerigar (parakeet). His daughter didn't look after it properly and he had threatened to give it away unless she showed more interest. She hadn't, so he'd brought the bird to see if there were any takers. Hannah was the only one who went to the cage and who was brave enough to want to touch the little bird, who was a deep, sea-turquoise blue with white and yellow tail feathers. He was really rather handsome but not used to being held, so he flapped around the cage before he could be caught and even then he tried his best to get out of the dad's firm grip. Once he was calmer and had stopped squawking, Hannah was allowed to stroke his tiny head and as soon as she touched him, he stopped flapping and stared at her, right in her eyes. They had an instant connection, even if it was just for a couple of seconds before he started struggling again and was placed back in his cage.

When Liz came to pick her up that afternoon after Girl Scouts, Hannah begged her mom to take the bird home.

At first, Liz was reluctant. She'd had budgies when she was a little girl and she loved them, but what about all the mess that came with them and the extra work? Hannah, of course, promised to look after the budgie and she was so insistent that Liz gave in. "Goodness knows what your dad will say when we come home with a bird!" she said, half-jokingly.

"He will be fine," said Hannah as she sat in the back seat and chatted softly to her new friend. She had her dad Ian wrapped around her little finger and Liz knew he was a softie when it came to animals, especially unwanted ones.

Her daughter was right. Although Ian scolded Liz for bringing another animal into the house, he liked the bird Hannah called Blu, partly after his colour but also after a character in one of her favourite movies, *Rio*.

Hannah wanted the bird to live in her bedroom, but Liz had her put his cage in the office until he settled down. For a few days, he was still very flighty and noisy, and it was clear that he hadn't been handled too much by his previous owners. For the first week, Hannah didn't even try to get him out of his cage. As soon as he seemed calmer, she put her hand in so that he could get used to her. Most of the time he flew around and clung to the bars, but a couple of times he did land on her hand. Encouraged, she did this several times a day, and slowly Blu settled down until, whenever she opened his cage, he would fly to the opening and hop right out onto her hand.

Hannah had read in one of her books that you can teach a budgie to talk, something Liz remembered all too well from her own experiences with her bird Joey, who she had taught to speak whole sentences. Together, Hannah and Liz sat with Blu and taught him to say basic expressions, such as "hello", "goodbye" and "how are you?" It was a process but, with patience, Blu did start to speak and Hannah was thrilled. It was the first time in forever that Liz had seen Hannah completely happy and absorbed. She kept a diary detailing her life with Blu and his achievements – having the little bird certainly enriched everyone's life.

"Blu was the best thing that had happened to Hannah in a very long time," says Liz. "He was a challenge at first because he didn't really like people that much, but his reluctance made her even more determined to gain his trust. He became her focus again. Whereas I think she had been so absorbed by the loss of her best friend, when Blu came along he gave her something to fill the time and her thoughts with, and she was never lonely again. It was such a pleasure to watch their friendship grow. From being really quite a nervous little bird, he would cling to the cage door when he heard her coming and squawk loudly to say hello – it was clear he was delighted to see her. I also enjoyed spending time with Hannah and Blu teaching him to talk – it took me right back to my childhood and my own budgie Joey. It made for some good bonding time for us all and I'm thankful for the quality time we spent together."

Blu became so tame that whenever Hannah let him out, she would stand in the middle of the room with her arm stretched out and he knew that was his signal, so he would fly to her and land on her hand.

They talked to each other all the time. Budgies can be incredibly vocal creatures and the pair would have conversations. Sometimes Blu would even try to copy what she was saying, much to Hannah's pride and amusement. When she did her homework, he would sit on the desk next to her and patter around. If he was close to Hannah, he was a content little bird. Often, he would sit on her shoulder like a king and go for a walk around the house without ever flying off.

The neighbourhood kids loved to see Blu and his tricks, so Hannah would often invite them in to watch his antics. This led to closer friendships and Hannah realized that she had other people she could hang out with who were just as fun to be around as Rachel had been. The bond she shared with Blu was something so special and unique. Blu clearly loved his human and Hannah adored him in return. She gave him the best care, love and attention and he gave his girl her life back in so many different ways.

"I am so glad that we took Blu home that day," says Liz. "They were meant to be together – of that I am sure. He came into Hannah's life right when she needed him – the timing couldn't have been more perfect. He brought so much more to her life than we could ever have imagined – he filled the void left by Rachel and he became Hannah's best friend. To see him get so excited when she would go to his cage was the best thing in the world. We all loved him."

Sadly, after two years, Blu died unexpectedly. Hannah found him in the bottom of the cage and the vet said he had probably suffered a heart attack, something budgies are prone to. His death devastated her and the whole family grieved. The house was suddenly very quiet, and Liz was so worried that Hannah would struggle to come to terms with her deep loss. Although she was sad for weeks, this time she had her neighbourhood friends to help fill the gap he left in her life. Thanks to Blu, she had connected with the local kids and they were good company.

Hannah will never forget Blu and the lessons he taught her. "I will probably miss Blu forever," Hannah says. "We had a connection I've never felt with another animal. He made me so happy and I know he loved me as much as I adored him. That day when he looked me straight in the eyes made me want him so badly. The way he stared at me so directly and intently – I felt something shift deep inside me. I had to take him home with me. I didn't want him to end up just anywhere because I knew I could give him a good life and the attention he so deserved. I'm glad I knew him, and I know how lucky we were to have the kind of relationship we did. Blu made everything right and I know that the last two years of his life were happy and fulfilled."

Chapter 17

DAVID AND JESS THE DOG

When Fiona turned 40, she decided that she wanted another child. She already had three girls – stepdaughter Lauren, and Sammie and Georgia, her kids with her husband Steve. Since her youth, she had wanted three biological kids – and with her body clock ticking, she thought this might be her last chance to fulfil her dreams.

Steve went along with the idea, even though he thought it was a bit mad, and not long after she turned 40 in March 2006, they started trying for a baby. Fiona's doctors had warned that, at her age, it might not happen. They advised her to try for a year and then, if no baby was conceived, just accept that it wasn't meant to be.

Far from it taking a long time, the opposite was true! Fiona conceived very quickly, and their son David was born weighing a very healthy 9 lb in April 2007.

"We couldn't believe that I got pregnant so quickly," recalls Fiona. "We were very lucky, and we were over the moon about it. My pregnancy went well but I was well aware that it was harder this time around, being that bit older. When David was born, the placenta ruptured and I haemorrhaged – it was touch and go for a while, but I pulled through, thank God. That's when I was sure that he was the last and I wouldn't go through a pregnancy ever again. We had a beautiful family and I had to be there to watch them grow up."

As the years went by and the kids grew older and started to do exams to go to university, Fiona and Steve realized that one day soon David would be like an only child, left alone in the house with his parents. He had a very close relationship with his sisters, but particularly Georgia, and his parents knew that he would miss all of them once they had moved out to start their own lives in a different town or city.

Growing up, Fiona had a corgi dog named Cindy and then a mongrel called Prudence. She also had two cats when she met Steve, but after they married and had a family they didn't have the time to care for a pet. Now, in advance of Georgia heading to university and David being on his own, she wondered if the moment was right to get a dog as a companion for her son, who had complained of being lonely. He missed the high-energy vibe that having a full house brought with it.

Fiona knew that he was unhappy and so she acted fast to alleviate the quietness that could envelop the house. Even with the best will in the world, having two parents in their fifties with major work commitments wasn't all that fun, Fiona knew, so she started to look for a dog. She registered with their closest shelter, the Bath Cats and Dog Home in south-west England, which was quite a stringent process as they were assessed for their suitability to adopt an animal.

They decided to look for something as small and active as a terrier, but when they paid a visit to the shelter to look at the dogs, one pup caught their attention when a lady walked by with a lurcher on a lead. The pretty girl had been found as a stray in Wiltshire and she was very nervous, so the shelter was looking for a home with no small children and no other animals. She was a bit of a sorry-looking pup, too. She was very thin, with her tail between her legs, and she didn't interact with anybody; rather, she cowered when she was given attention. It was clear that she had never experienced love or kindness in her short life because she didn't know how to react. The shelter believed that she had possibly been abandoned by travellers, who favoured the breed, but they didn't know why such a beautiful dog had been dumped.

Fiona liked the look of her and the family was invited back the next day to officially meet the dog, named Martha, but they were warned that she was very withdrawn and hadn't interacted with any families while she had been at the shelter. Georgia tagged along the next day, too, and to their surprise the pup didn't hide from anyone. She was definitely wary and nervous, but she did take a couple of treats from them before she let them stroke her pretty head.

The shelter lady was astonished. "You're the first people she has relaxed with," she said. The next day, they picked up the dog, who they renamed Jess, and took her home.

It took a good six weeks for Jess to completely settle into life with her new family. Fiona had bought her many toys but she didn't know how to play with them and she destroyed a lot of them. She would look at them blankly if someone threw a bone or a ball and she wouldn't touch anything unless she was told to. Without knowing her background, they could only assume that Jess, who was estimated to have been about a year old when she was rescued, had probably never had a family of her own, which was sad.

Gradually, they discovered Jess's little quirks, such as her being allergic to wet dog food, which meant they had to find her a palatable dry food. She was quite high-energy, and when she found her feet, she loved to play ball and chase around the garden. She also had a fear of white paper bags and preferred women to men.

Although she warmed to everyone, it was clear that David was her favourite and her very best buddy. Together, they would go for walks before and after school and she would sleep in his bedroom every night, all snuggled up together. She would sit by his side while he played the video game *Fortnite* and follow him everywhere, which he loved.

When the coronavirus pandemic struck and the world went into lockdown in the spring of 2020, Jess showed how much of an important part of the family she is. In fact, if it hadn't been for Jess, Fiona says that she doesn't know how any of them would have coped with not seeing family and friends for months.

"It was a very long few months of being in lockdown for David," says Fiona. "A teenage boy has to see his friends for his own mental well-being. While Georgia came home from university, she had a job making ice cream and wasn't laid off, so for most of the day, every day, David was stuck with me and Steve, which could have been potentially catastrophic if Jess hadn't been there. She kept us all in a routine, as she still had to be walked. So, rather than us all being stuck in the house for twenty-four hours a day going crazy, we took her out and got some exercise and lovely fresh air in our lungs, which is so good for the mind. Jess was wonderful company for David, who was on his own most of the day every day. Both Steve and I have a home office and remained busy during Covid-19, so David had to fend for himself a bit while we worked. In between his online schoolwork, he would play with her outside in the garden, something neither of them ever tired of. They would sit and have a break and share their lunch – it was touching to see them together so often."

While the future is uncertain because of the pandemic and its effects, one sure thing is that Jess has turned into an amazing rescue who is loved by her whole family. David no longer complains about feeling lonely because Jess is his constant companion who, particularly during lockdown, provided a structure and a purpose to his life.

"She is just an amazing dog," says Fiona. "I am so glad that we adopted her. She is the perfect match for David –

they are so alike. Both are tall and slim, and both have the gentlest, kindest personalities. I couldn't have hoped for a better outcome. I don't worry so much about David being an 'only child' now because he has Jess, the best friend he's ever had."

Chapter 18

MELANIE AND THE RESCUE PIGS

In the autumn of 2014, Melanie was so fed up of small-town living that she decided to make good on a lifelong dream to move to the country.

Melanie, her husband Tim and their kids Anna and Billy had lived in Plano, Texas for more than ten years, and in that time the place had grown very fast. In fact, it had grown so much that it didn't feel like home any more. There were so many new businesses and houses that Plano's community feel was gone and it seemed like just another town.

Melanie feared that if her kids grew up surrounded by so much industry, shops and people, they would miss out on the natural wonders that living in the country could give them. While Tim, a food-supply-chain consultant, was in agreement with the move, her kids did not want to leave their schools and friends, but Melanie was convinced that it was the right thing to do. She could feel it in her heart.

In May 2015, the family moved to Wills Point, Texas. They downsized into a house that, at 1,800 square feet, was 50 per cent smaller than the gorgeous home they left behind. The good thing about the house, and what made it appeal to Melanie and Tim, was that it was built on more than eight acres in the middle of nowhere. There was peace and quiet in abundance.

"I knew the children weren't happy with the move, so I tried to give them the best of both worlds," recalls Melanie. "Wills Point had a drill team, which was perfect for Anna, who was a dancer. There was also a golf team for my son and although we were in the middle of the country, we weren't that far from Wills Point town and the supermarkets, shops and entertainment. I fell in love with the place from the moment we saw the house – it was exactly what I had hoped to find. It fulfilled my dreams of leaving crowded Plano behind, as it was manageable for us as first-time landowners."

The family had the whole summer to settle in and Melanie bought some chickens for fresh eggs, a couple of goats and a horse for Anna, who had always loved horse riding.

One day, a family of what she thought were three wild pigs showed up and scared her, so she shooed them out of the gate and on their way. Being the soft-hearted lady she is, Melanie felt guilty that she hadn't helped the pigs, who had come onto her property rummaging for food, and she wanted to make amends somehow. She had never thought about having pigs, but seeing those three made her consider how it might be to rear pigs at her ranch. Surely it couldn't be that hard, she thought – don't pigs eat anything?

In September 2015, Melanie answered an advert for a couple of teacup piglets for sale on Facebook. They were advertised as being 11 weeks old and very cute. She met a man on the side of Highway 80, not far from her house, who gave her the adorable grey-and-white pigs in a reusable carrier bag. Melanie built a small pen outside the house for them and hoped for the best, not knowing that they were actually pot-bellied pigs and that they would grow enormously.

"After I had shut the gate on those wild pigs, I truly felt so bad that I hadn't even tried to help them," says Melanie. "I had never thought about owning pigs, but then I wanted to find some, as if to make it up to them. We called the piglets Pearl and Piglet, and we all took to them – they were so loving, sweet and cuddly. They made me fall madly in love with the idea of having more pigs. What I didn't know was that I was doing it all wrong. I fed them on bread, milk and pellets, which was actually too many rich foods for such tiny animals."

Sadly, Piglet died not long after. It was heartbreaking and, looking back, Melanie believes that when she got her she was barely six weeks old – and with the odds stacked against her because she was so young.

In January 2016, Melanie took in a pig called Buddy so that Pearl would have a friend. It was a disaster. Buddy would chase Pearl around all the time and he never gave her a minute's peace. Melanie, who thought he just wanted to play, locked him out so that he couldn't get near to Pearl. When she finally realized that he was constantly trying to mate with her, she built separate cages.

A few months later, Pearl disappeared. Melanie and the kids were terrified that she had got out and been eaten by a coyote, so they scoured the ranch looking for her. Eventually, they found her across the street in a pasture. She had made a little nest because she was in labour and was having piglets! Melanie bribed her out with strawberries and peppermints, and helped deliver Pearl's six babies in her bedroom.

"It was a train wreck," says Melanie. "I didn't know what to do to help her – I was in too deep. I did my best but she had one stillborn piglet and it broke my heart. I wondered if it was something that I had or hadn't done. I felt so responsible. The day after Pearl delivered, I got Buddy neutered and I built a huge pen in the barn for her and her babies. After five days in the bedroom, they moved into their new pen and I was determined to keep them safe no matter what. After that, I knew that I had to educate myself more about pigs otherwise I would make more mistakes. I knew that Pearl had been too young to have babies and it was my fault – I didn't want to make the same mistakes again. I reached into the community and joined a lot of support groups for pig owners on social media. I had fallen in love with the pigs and I wanted more, but I wanted to do it the right way."

For months, Melanie learned about keeping pigs and, while networking, she heard about so many unwanted pigs that needed homes because their owners lacked the correct knowledge to look after them. She met and heard about people who bought tiny teacup pigs who grew up to be much bigger animals that required extra care and space. This was a huge reason why they were suddenly homeless or sent to the abattoir. It was horrible and Melanie decide that she wanted to take in the unwanted pigs and either rehome them or keep them. She had the space and now she had the knowledge to care for them.

In August 2016, she picked up three pigs from a lady who needed someone to foster them. They were massive animals weighing 250 lb each; somehow, Melanie loaded them into her minivan and took them home. It was another learning process. Those pigs tried to eat Pearl and Buddy alive until she realized that there was an integration protocol that she had to carry out so that the new pigs would settle in with the others safely for the duration of their stay.

Her next try at fostering was Vlad, a nine-month-old grey and white pig who had been dumped by his family for growing too big. Vlad became good friends with Buddy, so Melanie kept him – he became her first successful adoption.

A little while later, she took in a massively overweight, 300-lb pig called Miss Tilly. Her elderly owner was very distressed because she was moving house and couldn't take her friend with her, so Melanie stepped in.

By December that year, she had taken in more rescues, including an adorable ten-week-old white and grey American pig called Walter, who had been given up by his owners because he had a peeing problem. Melanie picked him up from a parking lot in Plano and they bonded quickly. He became Melanie's first rescue that she raised as a house pig, and together they learned about potty-training and walking on a leash. She soon discovered he had a medical condition that caused his peeing problem and she raised him in diapers. He also had diabetes, so Melanie formulated a special diet to help keep his condition under control.

While Walter was a lot of work, he was Melanie's baby and wherever she went he would follow like a little puppy. He liked nothing more than curling up on her lap for snuggles at the end of the day and he loved to sleep close, but while he was definitely Melanie's boy, he integrated well with the other residents, too.

Melanie's name became well known in pig circles and before long she was inundated with requests from people who needed her help. Unwanted pigs were a huge problem in her area and there were few organizations that offered support.

A couple of days after Melanie got Walter, she received some unexpected and devastating news from her stepmother Linda. Her father John, whom she adored and was very close to, had died suddenly from a massive heart attack. After her parents had split up when she was a teenager, Melanie had lived with John and Linda for a few years. They lived on acreage and Melanie says it was there, sitting on the porch with her father in the evening sunlight, that her love of the countryside was cemented, and she had always vowed to have her own acreage when she got older.

"I spent many happy years with my dad," recalls Melanie. "He was everything to me. Even when I got married and settled down, we spoke all the time – I would turn to him when I needed advice or just a good laugh. He had been sick for a few years. He had gangrene years previously, which he miraculously survived, and then he was in a nursing home for the last part of his life, but he never lost his will to live a good life. I was so angry with God that he had survived against the odds when he got gangrene, only for him to die from a heart attack! It wasn't fair and he left a massive, gaping hole in my life that I couldn't come to terms with."

Melanie travelled to her father's funeral alone, leaving Tim and the kids to look after the ranch. She had no one else to care for her beloved animals, so she thought this was the best solution, but it caused a strain on her marriage. When she got home, Tim left her. She didn't hear from him for almost four months, then they had months of marriage counselling while Melanie took in more unwanted pigs. In 2017, despite her heartache, she took in 37 more pigs.

Later that year, she received her non-profit status and My Pig Filled Life was born. Melanie's home was officially a pet rescue and her dreams were coming true, despite all her personal problems.

Tim did eventually return to the family home in January 2018, but their problems were too deep-rooted and after another year and a half of turmoil, they split up for good and were finally divorced.

"When Tim left me, I was in a terribly delicate state emotionally," recalls Melanie. "I'd just lost Dad and I never thought I'd come to terms with losing him. I needed Tim to hold me up and tell me it was going to be okay. He couldn't do that. Over the next few months, a lot of hurt came out. Tim was so jealous of my work with the pigs. I guess he felt second best and neglected by me. Maybe he was right, I don't know. My priorities did change with the rescue, though – I admit that much. But I also thought our priorities were the same. I learned that he hated the pigs peeing over the house, that I didn't have as much time for us as a couple. He didn't like that we could never go away on holiday – we couldn't travel because I couldn't leave the animals. Maybe the split was as much my fault as it was his."

Sadly, at a time when she needed her husband the most, she felt he wasn't there and Melanie found another source of support – her rescue pigs.

In her first year of being a bona fide rescue, she took in many pigs and their babies. There was Lolly with her seven piglets, there were Charlotte and Ore, and there was also an underweight piglet called Spanky who just wanted to be loved. Melanie also worked with her local animal shelter on a major cruelty case where she took in 55 pigs, and there have been many more since.

During her marriage troubles and her grief, her pigs gave her the support she needed to make it through.

"My rescue pigs gave me all the love and support I needed to get stronger," says Melanie. "If it hadn't been for them,

I don't know what I would have done. I just know I would have gone under. Every day I would sit outside with the pigs, rubbing their bellies, building strong bonds. I would cry to them and talk to them when I was having a bad day and they would listen without judgment as I poured my heart out. They made me get up every day because I had a commitment to them. If I hadn't, I might have stayed in bed all day, really depressed. They gave me the best reason to get over my emotional pain and forge ahead with a new life. I accepted what my husband said and that our marriage was over. My rescues gave me the confidence and the drive to carry on, no matter how sad I was."

Melanie now lives with her 284 pigs and to date she has rescued 383 pigs. She has a team of volunteers who help her, and she works with many different animal-rescue organizations all over the state.

"Pigs are much more intellectual and emotional than a lot of people give them credit for," says Melanie. "They cry, they feel grief just like humans and they easily pick up on my moods. I sit with them for hours in the pasture on a blanket and they come over for a cuddle or a belly rub. They expect nothing but they give so much more than I ever expected. I can't ever imagine my life without a pig – that's something I would never have said about a man. Yes, it was devastating when my husband and I split up, but I got over it. I would never get over losing my rescues. It is the most amazing feeling in the world to be able to wrap your arms around a pig. This was the life I was meant to lead, and I won't give the pigs up for anything or anybody. They're here to stay because they save me every day from being lonely and sad. I could never be depressed with my pigs – they give me everything to survive for."

Chapter 19

RACHEL AND THE DOGS PATTY AND BONNIE

From the age of just 11 years old, Rachel suffered with depression. She had been a figure skater for several years and the sport had been demanding. Her coach was tough on her and she was taught that showing emotion was weak.

As an only child, Rachel was hard on herself and even though her parents Karen and Brian never put her under any pressure to do well, she was always determined to be the best. In middle school, in Florida, she was bullied. Boys and girls teased Rachel about her nose – she was called "Pinocchio", "big nose" and even "ugly". There was a lot of whispering and laughing about and at her during class and lunch, and poor Rachel was desperately unhappy. She didn't talk about it with her parents and she made up excuses about why she couldn't go to school.

By the time she was 16, her depression was such a problem that she was having therapy sessions on and off, and her doctor prescribed medication to help with her feelings of despair.

"Looking back, I wonder if the start of my depression was the ice skating," says Rachel. "It is obviously a one-person sport, so I demanded a lot of myself to do well. If I did so or not, it was all on me. I rarely showed emotion, which is also a bit of a family trait. I bottled all my worries and problems up inside rather than speaking to my parents or my friends. I thought I should be able to handle anything. As I grew older and I went to college, I put myself under so much unnecessary pressure. I took on more work than I needed to, and this not only made my depression worse, but it also caused extreme anxiety. It got to the point where I dropped out of my junior year because I couldn't handle the pressures any more. Luckily, I had done extra studies at high school, so I was still able to graduate, but it was a really difficult time."

Rachel had always longed to study abroad, so when she graduated in December 2017, she thought it was the perfect time to put a plan in action. Deciding to leave the country and go it alone without her parents was a big decision, but she felt that her depression and anxiety was relatively under control, so she signed up with an Australian organization. The company pairs up volunteers of all ages with programmes all over the world. The whole trip is arranged by professionals to ensure a safe and rewarding experience.

Rachel, who wants to be a social worker, signed up to work in a convent in Peru with mentally disabled children, and in March 2018 she flew out to the city of Cusco to start.

Unfortunately, it was incredibly emotionally demanding, and she found the whole situation there heartbreaking. There were not enough volunteers to help all of the children, who slept together in king-size beds and had little privacy. They were left for hours each day in soiled diapers and they had little interaction with the outside world, apart from a physiotherapist, who was overworked, and a few volunteers like Rachel.

"I hated it," recalls Rachel. "I had thought it might help me realize my dream to become a social worker, but it was a terrible experience and not something that I had expected. Although they had a roof over their heads and were fed, there was never enough time to do the job well because there were too many of them who needed round-the-clock attention. I couldn't cope emotionally with what I saw. It preyed on my mind and I couldn't get the pictures of those poor children out of my dreams. I knew that if I carried on volunteering it would be really bad for my mental state."

When Rachel had landed in Peru and taken a taxi to her host family's house in Cusco, she had been aware of the large amount of dogs living on the streets in the city. The problem wasn't just confined to the city, either. Every night as she lay in her bed, she could hear dogs crying and digging through dustbins trying to find food, and animals fighting.

She had always had a particular fondness for dogs, having grown up with a rescue dog at home, so she decided to change her volunteer status and find a dog shelter where she could work instead. Her search led her to the Cusco

Protección de Animales dog shelter. The building is set on three levels carved into the side of a mountain and its owner, Mila, welcomed Rachel's help with open arms.

Rachel discovered that dogs are considered to be no better than rats in Peru. It is custom to buy an adorable puppy from the pet store, but owners do not pay for them to be spayed or neutered since it's expensive. When the dogs are fully grown and not as cute or are too large to handle, they are tossed out into the streets to fend for themselves. They breed and add to the numbers of stray animals, so some people put poison down to get rid of them. It's a desperately sad situation and there's not much help in Peru for the street dogs.

Those at Mila's shelter, however, enjoy a life in a doggy paradise. They are not kept in cages or tied up; instead, they are encouraged to roam freely in the woods and fields that the property is built on. These are the lucky ones, plucked from the streets and from cruel owners. They are given dog food, chicken livers and rice every day, and if they can't be adopted they will live the rest of their days with Mila.

Rachel's role at the shelter was to help at feeding times, organize and attend local spay and neuter events and, very importantly, to love the residents and play with them in the fields. The task was an easy one and she adored being around the animals. While she was there, she fell in love with a beautiful black and sandy coloured girl called Patricia, or Patty for short, who was thought to be part hound.

Patty had been in the shelter for about a year and a half after she had been found with her sister Bonnie on the streets.

She was very sick with stage-three distemper and Mila didn't know if she would survive. Thankfully, she did, but it left her with a mild neurological impairment, which causes her back paw to twitch every now and again. Not long after she got better, she was adopted by a family and Mila though it was the last she would see of her.

A few months later, Mila called the new family to check on Patty, only to be told that she had gone missing and they hadn't been able to find her because they had moved away. Mila was distraught but there was nothing that could be done. Not long after, a tourist called the shelter. He had found a stray dog; when he sent a photograph to Mila, it was Patty! By some kind of a miracle, she had been found but she was severely traumatized and desperately sad.

When Rachel first arrived at the shelter, she saw Patty sitting on a sofa all alone. She looked so frail and upset, so she gently sat next to her and stroked her soft, furry head. The little dog didn't move but she did look at Rachel with the most soulful eyes she had ever seen.

Patty had come back to Mila pregnant and, as sad as it sounds, it was considered to be the best for her to be booked in to have an abortion and spay surgery. Rachel, who had really taken to the pretty little dog, was allowed into the surgery with Patty and afterwards she was put into her arms for her to take back to the shelter.

"Poor Patty was very sick on the way home and so I comforted her as best as I could," recalls Rachel. "Again, Mila wasn't sure if she would make it, but I was determined that she was going to survive. I stayed with her as much as I could while she recovered, and she really took to me. She would get excited to see me and shower me with kisses. I looked forward to seeing her – she made my heart leap with absolute pure, unbridled joy."

One of the things that her parents had made her promise not to do before she went to Peru was bring home a dog. They had read about students going away during gap years and then coming home with a pet. But even with this in mind, Rachel knew that she couldn't leave Patty behind when she returned to America in June. The dog had been through so much in her short life that Rachel couldn't leave her again. Using money from bonds her grandparents gave her, Rachel paid around $1,500 in airline fees and vaccinations to take Patty home with her. It was money well spent and Patty settled into life in the US beautifully.

Rachel stayed in regular touch with Mila and she was dismayed when Mila told her that a woman had backed out of adopting Bonnie, Patty's sister. Bonnie was as sweet and gentle as her sister, although she looked more like a black Labrador than a hound dog. To look at them together, you wouldn't know that they were related, but all the time in the shelter they had stuck together.

When Rachel heard about Bonnie, her plight preyed on her mind. This was Patty's sister, not just any other dog, and she deserved the kind of life that Patty now enjoyed. Rachel decided that she wanted her, particularly when Mila sent pictures of her looking sad and dejected at the shelter. She launched a successful Go Fund Me appeal to raise funds to bring Bonnie to America, and when she came home, no one was happier than Patty to see her sister. They enjoyed the happiest of reunions.

Since the girls came into her life, Rachel's mental health has improved enormously. She has weaned herself off her medication and has moved back to university to do her master's degree – this is the first time she has ever lived alone. She now views her life in two halves: the one before Peru, which was blighted by mental-health issues, and the one after, where she is more positive and in control of everything that she wants to do.

"Patty and Bonnie have had such a positive effect on my emotional stability," says Rachel. "They have given me such purpose. When I have a difficult day and I want to stay in bed, unlike before I can't do that now. I have to get up to feed them and walk them. I don't have the luxury of giving in to my emotions and spending my time moping in my room. If I don't care for them, they would have no one, and coming from the streets, I never want them to have to experience anything like that again. I am their everything and, honestly, they are my everything, too. As an only child, I like being around people, but I am also happy to be by myself. It isn't a lonely experience because wherever I am, my girls are, too. They instinctively know when I need a pick-up. If I'm miserable, they both go out of their way to play with me. They're more rambunctious and I know it's because they want to take my mind off whatever is troubling me."

Rachel remains deeply grateful: "I think that, as much as I have helped my dogs, they have saved me, too. It is hard to be consumed and feel bad about yourself when you have to be focused on their well-being. My life after Peru is like a rebirth. Having Patty and Bonnie has helped me to get my priorities in order, to get my mind and my life straight. I am stronger because of them – their love is powerful, and I am thankful fate brought us together."

Chapter 20

HELEN AND RUSSELL THE CROW

Ever since childhood, Helen has had a fascination with birds. In her dreams, she could fly with them and at school she would write stories and draw intricate pictures of her favourite breeds.

When she was a teenager, she would rescue pigeons she found in the street near her home in Gloucestershire in the south-west of England. Her mum Julie let her keep them in a small shed in the back garden so that she could rehabilitate them. Some of them were injured after falling from their nests in the trees and others were abandoned by their mothers. Usually, after three or four months of love and care, the pigeons were able to be released back into the wild and Helen's work was done. She loved being with the birds and her work was very rewarding.

"I was obsessed with birds when I was a kid," recalls Helen. "There was something about them, the way they could fly up high, so beautiful and peaceful. I think I secretly wished that I was a bird. I wasn't afraid of them like some people are. To me, it was the most natural thing in the world to hold a flapping bird in my hands, to look it in the eyes and make a contact – a bond with them – even if they were wild. Mum said I had a gift and she encouraged me to save them. I would walk down the street and see them lying there, pitiful, having fallen out of their nests and unable to get back to their family. A lot of people consider crows and pigeons to be like vermin, so they don't help, but to me all the birds were beautiful, and I wanted to save them."

Helen lost count of the number of pigeons she rescued over the years. Even when she met and married her husband Tristan, her love for birds continued and he supported her endeavours to make a difference.

In spring 2016, she was walking dogs for a friend one day when she spotted a small black bird all huddled up in the doorway of a restaurant on a busy street. It was very still and was squawking softly as if it were calling for help. The poor thing couldn't have been more than a week or two old, Helen estimated, and was all alone with no sign of a nest or parents. It was a miracle she had even spotted it as it was so small. Helen gently scooped it up and it fitted in the palm of her hand. She didn't know what kind of a bird it was – all that mattered was getting it to safety. She later found out that the bird she named Russell Crow was indeed a crow. He had inverted feet, a fractured femur, stunted growth and weak, brittle feathers, which meant that he couldn't fly.

Helen, who was now an experienced dog trainer and pet behaviourist, hadn't taken in any birds for a couple of years. Instead, she would give any she found to the local countryside charity to rehabilitate them. But she knew that if she took Russell to them, they would probably euthanize him because he was considered to be disabled. If the bird couldn't be released back into nature, then this was often the only solution. Helen couldn't stand the thought of anything happening to Russell so, with Tristan's support, she kept him in a large parrot cage in their house. The cage door was never closed so he had the freedom to roam around the house whenever he chose. It became his place of safety when he wanted to sleep or be alone, and he became attached to Helen like she was his mate. He often also slept in her and Tristan's bedroom or stayed in there at night if Helen went to bed early, and he settled in quickly. That's when he really began to rule the roost and a few unforeseen, quite major problems cropped up.

He suffered from severe separation anxiety when she left the room or the house and this manifested in him screaming the place down – the noise was excruciating, and he literally wouldn't stop until she returned. Then he would attack Tristan and peck his arm if he went too near to Helen. It was his way of saying that he was the one who was looking after Helen – she didn't need a human because she had Russell. It was a huge problem and Tristan, who was patient and understanding, got hurt many times.

"When you get a bird from a young age, they can become tame and Russell definitely imprinted on me," says Helen.

"He didn't see me as a human or the person who cared for him, he saw me as his equal and, as such, his mate. It was an unusual situation. His bond with me was tight and I wouldn't have had it any other way, but the relationship was problematic as he couldn't bear it when I left a room or even went to the toilet! I wasn't sure what to do. I couldn't have Tristan getting hurt, so I spoke with a fellow animal behaviourist who suggested we desensitize him by building an aviary in the garden where he could spend most of his time with other birds."

Tristan constructed a beautiful aviary in their backyard and it prompted Helen to set up her own bird rescue as she thought it would be good for Russell to have the company of his own species, too. In 2017, Russell's Rescue was born.

Since then, Helen has taken in hundreds of birds, mostly rooks, crows, jackdaws and magpies, and the majority of them are disabled and can't be released. She works with other animal rescues in her area who bring her any birds that are injured and that can be saved. Helen is well known for her expertise and she receives requests for help all the time.

The rescue now boasts three aviaries – one for the disabled birds, another for the life-timers and a third for the ones who will be released back into nature. Russell is mostly content living with his other special friend Pip, a fellow rook – so long as he gets his time inside the house with his "mate" Helen, which includes sleepovers every night, regular baths, pecking the toilet rolls and mealtimes eating his favourite baby foods.

Time spent with Russell is precious to Helen, too. He has become more than just a rescued bird – he has become a best friend who has given back to Helen in so many ways as she continues a recovery from eating disorders and mental-health problems.

In 2014, when Helen was 18 and at college, she developed body dysmorphic disorder, a chronic mental illness that involves a person's obsessive focus on a perceived flaw in their appearance. For Helen, it was mostly with her figure, and she started to lose weight, which led to anorexia and bulimia – at her lowest, she weighed just seven stone, which for her 5 feet 7 inches in height was far too light. She was skin and bone but, at the time, she couldn't see it.

She believes that she developed both disorders after being teased at school because she was so tall and heavy. One day, after a school weigh-in, the nurse flippantly told Helen that she was the heaviest in the class, and it stuck with her.

In addition, she has also suffered from obsessive-compulsive disorder on and off for years, which manifested as a severe form of checking things. So, every so often, it also raises its ugly head and she has days when she has to check everything, including Russell.

Helen works from home now, particularly since the Covid-19 pandemic struck, and she does get lonely, particularly when Tristan is out. Russell is her rock in times like these and he has the ability to avert a stressful situation. When she's having a bad day, Helen sits with Russell on her shoulder and he gently pecks her ear to let her know she is not alone. He loves to play with her hair because, in his mind, he is grooming his mate.

"I think I relapse with the OCD maybe once a week and it's usually something to do with Russell, like I've not locked the cage or something, or I haven't turned off the hair straighteners," says Helen. "The anorexia and bulimia is under control but there are times when I eat way too much and then I cut back on what I eat for a few days after. Like any mental disorder, it has to be kept under control and that can be a difficult thing to do, particularly at times of stress. I'm definitely not as bad as I used to be, but it is still there if I let it crowd my thoughts. Having Russell around really takes my mind off things one hundred per cent, and by focusing on him I feel better quickly."

Russell raises Helen's spirits with his comical antics. He loves to steal the remote control and credit cards. He shouts out "whatcha got" and sings "hello" all the time, which just melts everyone's hearts. Helen has trained him to play a game where she tells him the colour of a card in a basket and he picks it out from a deck. They spend a lot of time doing puzzles, chasing balls and singing together, and Russell enjoys watching the TV at night. She loves to take his picture, as well as selfies, when he's on her shoulder, and he poses like a magazine star! Helen swears that he is more intelligent than any dog she has worked with and reckons he has the mind of a three-year-old child. Without Russell, Helen says she wouldn't be complete.

"Russell is the most important thing in my life," says Helen. "I would say even more than my husband, but in a different way, and Tristan understands my deep love for Russell. He makes the bad times good and the good times even better. He means so much to me and I know he won't be here forever – rooks can live for twenty years – so I'm making the most of each day by creating memories. We bring the best out in each other. He gets naturally unsettled and anxious sometimes and I instinctively know when it's happening, so I have him in the house with me and I help him through his anxiety, just like he helps me. We are a wonderful team, and we rescue each other every day. Russell really is an enigma. He came from such a poor beginning and he has embraced his new life with me, Tristan and the other birds – he inspires us both to live our best lives no matter what."

Chapter 21

ALEX AND MORTIMER THE GUINEA PIG

It was a tiny hamster called Pipsqueak who inspired Alex and Jason's love for all things rodent. It was May 2012 and the summer before Alex started undergrad law school. She and Jason had started dating that year and they wanted their own pet.

They found Pipsqueak at the Bloomington Animal Shelter in Indiana, and as soon as they saw the perfect, sable-coloured hamster, they agreed to give him his forever home. Except the brown hamster with the golden rings around its eyes and curls behind its ears wasn't a boy but a very sweet girl who, unbeknown to them, was quite ill.

As soon as they got her home, Alex thought she smelled a little "off" and a visit to the vets showed up a urinary infection that took some months to clear up. When Pipsqueak was feeling better, the couple took her everywhere with them so she wouldn't ever feel alone. She went in the car, on walks in

Alex's pocket and to visit friends. She became quite the little celebrity and Alex loved her like family.

"Pipsqueak really stole our hearts," says Alex. "She was such a pretty, dainty little girl with tons of personality who I know loved us right back. She would squeak with delight when she saw us and she enjoyed going out and meeting other people. She inadvertently became the ultimate accessory and people loved her. I adored my little friend and I just wanted to keep her safe with us forever."

Sadly, about a week into Alex starting law school, Pipsqueak fell ill again. Alex got up to go to class one morning and found her dying in her cage. She called the emergency vet but, before she could get an answer, Pipsqueak died in her hands. It was incredibly sad and the couple grieved for their lost girl who, in such a short period of time, had left such an impact on their lives. To help deal with their loss, Alex adopted five more hamsters who needed homes because of sickness and surrender by their owners when they couldn't look after them any more.

In March 2013, Alex woke up in the middle of the night with an idea inspired by Pipsqueak.

"I told Jason that I wanted to set up a little organization called The Pipsqueakery, named after our girl," says Alex. "I thought we could take in unwanted hamsters and nurse them back to health and either keep or rehome them. I had realized that there wasn't a place to send hamsters with medical needs and the thought of them being euthanized because they couldn't get the care that they required broke my heart. So we bought more cages and started to look for unwanted hamsters in the local newspaper listings and Craigslists. It was amazing how quickly word spread that we had set up The Pipsqueakery. For the next two years, we were incredibly busy."

In February 2014, Alex was contacted by a lady from Chicago who had 21 pregnant hamsters. It was a mammoth undertaking, but The Pipsqueakery pulled it off. Many lives were saved and later sent to loving homes in Michigan, Kentucky, Pennsylvania and other states. Then a lady from New York contacted The Pipsqueakery. Her two hamsters had bred, coincidentally, 21 babies and she didn't know what to do – there was no way she could keep and look after so many young. Without hesitation, Alex said she would have them and, luckily, by this stage, the babies hadn't bred, so their rescue was an easy one. The lady even drove them from New York to ensure their safety.

In 2015, Alex graduated from law school and moved into a new house with a basement so that she and Jason could expand The Pipsqueakery. Together, they took in more hamsters, as well as rats and gerbils, and were busier than ever before. Somehow, they managed to look after the rodents in between their full-time jobs, and, although stressful at times, it was worth the reward.

Through Pipsqueak, Alex's life had changed so much for the better and she didn't think she would know another love like the one she felt for her first hamster – until February 2017, when a Craigslist advert caught her eye.

A woman was trying to find a new home for a blind, deaf and diseased five-week-old guinea pig. She didn't want the hassle of a sick animal but thankfully she tried to rehome him. Alex wasn't close to where the albino white guinea pig was, so she asked a volunteer friend to go to pick him up. But, that same night, the poor little guy started having seizures, so Alex instructed her friend to take him to the emergency vet in South Bend, Indiana. The guinea pig almost died but, by some miracle, he managed to survive the night.

Alex met her friend halfway to pick up him up and when she finally saw him, she was shocked. He weighed just 76 grams and was so small he fitted in the palm of her hand. It turned out the guinea pig, whom she named Mortimer, had the "lethal white" genetic disease, which means that he was born without any skin pigmentation. This condition can cause a whole host of problems: many lethal white guinea pigs are smaller and skinnier than their peers, they are often blind and/or deaf and they almost all have teeth problems, including missing incisors and deformed molars. Poor Mortimer couldn't eat because he was born with just one top incisor and a few overgrown molars. Alex kept him in bed with her and Jason at night and fed him a liquid diet of baby food and butternut squash.

It took a solid three months for Mortimer to put on weight and start to thrive. By this time, although Alex was highly allergic to his fur, she was head over heels in love with the little chap. Even though he was small at just 600 grams fully grown, he had a huge personality and an attitude to match.

"Mortimer would talk to us a lot," recalls Alex. "He was so loud sometimes. As soon as he would hear or sense me, he would shout with excitement at the top of his little voice. We got a tiny pushchair and we took him for walks in our neighbourhood. If he wasn't in the pushchair, he was in a baby carrier in my arms and he would literally go everywhere with us. We took him to the grocery store, to the park, out for walks down the street and I think we even took him to the police station once. I believe that the highlight of his day was being out in the fresh air making new friends. He brought so many people so much joy. They couldn't help but smile and stroke him when they saw him, and he lapped it up. I loved being his mom – we shared a unique bond."

When Mortimer turned a year old, Alex held a birthday party for him, and she live-streamed it from The Pipsqueakery Facebook page. After that, he had gifts sent to him from all over the world.

It turns out that Mortimer appeared in Alex's life when she needed him the most. She was incredibly stressed out in her job as a lawyer and she had problems with bringing her work home with her and not being able to switch off from it in the evenings. At the same time, she was seeing so many animal-cruelty cases, and taking in record numbers of hamsters, gerbils and guinea pigs, that it was a struggle to stay positive and to recognize the good that she was doing. It caused Alex a lot of anxiety and her main comfort was Mortimer, who would sit with her for hours and suck her fingers like a baby. They would snooze together on the sofa and he would purr contentedly as she stroked his back, which in turn relaxed Alex, too.

"I found it hard to see how much human cruelty there was against the animals," says Alex. "We saw it every day and it was depressing that the rodents we took in were treated so horribly. It weighed heavy on my mind and sometimes I would have a good old cry about people's negligence and cruelty. I couldn't understand how they could hurt an innocent creature. Mortimer was definitely my comfort. I would come home from work and play with him or watch him from the office on a baby monitor – whatever was happening, I couldn't help but smile at him. He made my days more bearable and looking at his sweet little face was a constant reminder that The Pipsqueakery was worth all the blood, sweat and tears that we put into it. I hadn't loved another one like that since Pipsqueak but there was something about this gutsy, clever, ballsy little guinea pig that I admired so much. When I needed a little bit of that white personality, he never let me down."

Unfortunately, lethal white guinea pigs don't tend to live as long as their peers and in May 2018 Mortimer passed away after a two-month upper-respiratory infection turned into pneumonia. Devastated, Alex stayed in bed, barely functioning as she grieved her deep loss. The house felt so quiet without her chatterbox, and even though she was surrounded by all of her other rescues, she longed for Mortimer's company.

It was during a quiet time of contemplation that she had another brilliant idea. In memory of Mortimer, she decided to expand The Pipsqueakery and take up the cause of saving more lethal whites. Since then, The Pipsqueakery has rescued these guinea pigs from all over the United States and even from Canada. Their work is well known in animal-rescue circles and, to date, they have saved more than 30 lethal whites and 2,000 animals in total.

While Alex is still a lawyer, which pays some of the bills, Jason is responsible for the full-time running of The Pipsqueakery, where no rodent is turned away, no matter what condition or illness it is suffering from. It's home to special-needs animals from across the country, many with missing limbs, heart disease, neurological problems or suffering from seizures.

Alex and Jason's house has been overrun by the demand while they raise money to build a permanent facility, so, in the meantime, they have had to expand into their bedroom, where they have 21 bunnies in residence. There's never a dull moment but Alex and Jason wouldn't have their lives any other way now. The Pipsqueakery is more than a rescue; it's their vocation and they take it very seriously. But always in Alex's mind are Pipsqueak and Mortimer, the unforgettable hamster and guinea pig who inspired her to go big with her dreams and to keep going during tough times.

"Those two will always have a piece of my heart," Alex says. "They were such characters who fought to survive, and they remind me every day to keep fighting for the animals, no matter what hurdles I come across. Mortimer in particular helped my anxiety so much. He was like a ray of sunlight who lit up the room whenever he was there. Just holding him close was a tonic to me – he always made me feel better. I would say that every rescue has a positive effect on me and Jason. The cuddles, the happiness and the love they show us – well, I doubt we would find that anywhere else and we feel privileged to be able to help them. They let me close the door on my stressful 'everyday' life when I come home, and there's no doubt they make me a better person. I'm lucky to be the one who helps to look after these amazing creatures."

Chapter 22

LAURA AND ANGEL THE HORSE

As Laura looked over the stable door, a pair of sunken black eyes stared at her from the corner. Their gaze belonged to a black horse who had been taken in by the rescue barn where Laura had just taken a trail ride.

"We don't know what to do with her," her new owner explained. "We rescued her forty-eight hours ago and she won't eat or interact with us. No one can even get near her."

Laura, who had no experience of being around horses apart from a couple of trail rides, felt drawn to the animal, who looked so sad. She knew she probably shouldn't, but she wanted to pet her. As she leaned over the door, the horse walked slowly toward her. "Hello, lamb, how are you?" said Laura softly as she gently stroked the mare's face. The owner was astonished as the horse nuzzled Laura. She agreed that Laura could take her out of her stall and, even more incredibly, the mare let her groom her while she ate a bucket of food.

"It was surreal," recalls Laura. "I had always been fascinated by horses and when I saw Angel, I had to get to know her. There was something about this girl that pulled me in. I wasn't afraid of her even though she had not let anyone at the barn touch her. When I saw those eyes, I knew she wouldn't hurt me. It's still hard to explain, but I just knew that I was meant to meet her."

Originally from Scotland, Laura and her then husband Derek and her parents Diane and Hughie had moved to Florida in 2006, where they ran several holiday-management companies. Like many expats, they moved to America for a better standard of life with more opportunities, but with that came long, 18-hour days working behind a desk, and Laura piled on the pounds.

Given that it was cheaper to eat out most nights and there were fast-food joints on every corner, Laura's weight ballooned until she was 350 lb. While the businesses were successful, it was a lonely existence and Laura felt unhealthy and ashamed of herself, yet she was caught in a trap of working with little time for anything else.

For Christmas 2009, Derek bought her a package of three trail rides at a local barn, which was also a rescue and rehabilitation centre. While she was thrilled with her gift, she was also nervous and worried that they wouldn't have a horse big enough to carry her. They did have a big stocky horse, but she felt conspicuous.

"I was so excited to go and ride a horse, but I was also embarrassed because I was so big," remembers Laura. "I had visions of me getting to the barn and them not having a horse strong enough to carry me. Thankfully that didn't happen, and the barn owner told me that the horse they put me on was definitely strong enough to carry me, but I was aware that I was so much bigger than anyone who was there that day. However, I really enjoyed the ride once I managed to put my worries aside and I couldn't wait to go back. Being out in the fresh air away from my stuffy office was very freeing for me."

The next week, Laura and Diane went for another trail ride and, as they walked around the barn, the owner told them the story of Angel, their latest rescue. Angel was one of nine thoroughbred mares who had been sold by a famous racing stables to one of their agents, who wanted to set up his own racing business. Sadly, in the 2008 economic crash, he lost a lot of money and he couldn't afford to run his barn any longer, so the horses were left out to pasture with no food or care. Florida's animal services had got involved and Angel was sent to DreamCatcher rescue ranch, where Laura was having her trail rides, while it was decided what to do with the horse.

After she had managed to get the mare to eat, Laura couldn't get her out of her mind. She thought about her all the time, so much so that she decided that she wanted to buy her. Laura called the rescue centre and told the owner that she wanted to buy Angel, who said no because, at just 850 lb, she was way too small for Laura to ride.

"The lady was very subtle, but I knew what she meant," says Laura. "She meant I was too overweight for the horse and it stung because there was nothing I wanted more than that horse. However, I had no plans right then to ride her; I just wanted to groom her, spend time with her and to walk her around on a lead rope. Looking back, I guess I just wanted to make a difference in her life, to show her what love is. I know it sounds crazy that I would want her, but she had stolen my whole heart. I had never felt like that toward an animal but my depth of feeling for her was so deep already. I needed Angel in my life."

Laura paid the adoption fee of $1,500 and she spent every day she could at the barn interacting with Angel. They quickly bonded and time spent with her was a welcome release from Laura's work commitments.

The barn was also a riding school and Laura sometimes watched students taking their lessons. A sweet lady once said to Laura, "You will ride your horse one day," and that set off a burning desire in her heart to learn to ride. Her only obstacle was her weight, and even though Angel was steadily getting heavier as she grew stronger, Laura was still much too big for her to carry her safely.

Laura realized that the only way she was going to achieve her dream of riding Angel was to lose a significant amount of weight. She had accepted her size for too long – now she was determined to change. She joined several different slimming groups and, although it was a hard slog because she had to change so many bad eating habits, she lost more than

50 lb in the first six months. By this time, Angel was 1,100 lb, which meant that she could carry Laura.

"I had waited for the day to come when I could ride my horse for so long, yet when it did, I was terrified," says Laura. "I was still very heavy and I didn't want to hurt my baby. I remember I put my foot in the stirrup and I hovered over her back wanting to cry before I lowered myself very gently into the saddle. She didn't flinch at all, but it was always in the back of my mind that I was heavier than I wanted to be. Yet walking around riding *my* girl was such an uplifting experience and I felt fantastic. I vowed to lose more weight so that I could eventually take lessons and ultimately take her to horse shows. Angel gave me big dreams to do things that I never would have thought about. All I knew was that when I was with her, or when I rode her, I was calmer and happier than I ever was away from her."

Their first showjumping competition was around 18 months after Laura had adopted Angel, and it was a big local event attended by many riders of all ages. Laura, who was at this time about 250 lb, competed in several jumping classes and while she and Angel did well and won ribbons, it was also one of the worst experiences of her life.

A group of mothers whose kids were competing got together and they reported Laura to the show office for neglect and abuse because, they said, she was too fat to ride Angel. Several members of the show team had to investigate their complaint and they found Laura and her teacher at the showground barn with the horses. In front of everyone, they grilled them both about Angel, and after hearing their story of how she had been rescued and was quite capable of carrying Laura, they dismissed the complaint.

The problem was that everyone on the showground heard about it and Laura gained a kind of notoriety that wasn't fair or just. She felt that everywhere she rode, people stared and talked about her.

"When those people told me that there had been a complaint about me and what had been said, I was just so horribly embarrassed," says Laura. "At that moment I wanted the ground to swallow me and Angel up in it. I had never been so humiliated. I wanted to run away it was so awful with those women staring at me. I wasn't too heavy for Angel and the show runners knew that, but it didn't stop people gossiping about us. The show was ruined for me, but when we got back to the barn I looked at Angel and I knew then that I wasn't going to be beaten. 'We're going to prove them all wrong,' I told her, and that was my next weight-loss goal."

When she lived in Scotland, Laura had enjoyed Muay Thai boxing classes and they had helped to keep her fit. She knew that dieting alone wasn't going to help her shift more weight, so she joined a boxing gym where she lost more than 60 lb and inches off her waist. During this time, she still took Angel to horse shows but she was often discriminated against for her size. It was often clear that while she should have won a ribbon, she was overlooked – sometimes she would ride beautiful, clear rounds and wouldn't even place. It was disheartening, but Laura was determined. On the difficult days, Angel instinctively knew that she was upset and would nuzzle her gently on her face as if to say "I love you", and the tight bond they shared gave her the will to carry on.

Laura's next weight-loss target was to be able to compete in a special riding coat called a shadbelly, which dressage riders typically wear. It is a black coat with long tails and a much shorter, buttoned front. Laura was determined to flatten her belly enough so that she could wear it proud – and that's exactly what she did. Within two and a half years, and despite some weight fluctuations, Laura was down to just under 180 lb. She rode Angel all the time, so she kept fit and she felt the healthiest she had done for many years.

In 2012, she decided that she wanted Angel in her own backyard, so the family bought a large piece of land in Groveland, Florida, where they built a barn. Laura lived in one house on the site and her parents in another. Laura's aim was to carry on working while providing rescue and rehabilitation for unwanted and neglected horses. Inspired by her own rescue Angel, it became more of a vocation. She named her barn Dark Horse Stables after Angel and the other horses, but also after herself, the "dark horse" who managed to make a comeback when everything felt like it was against her.

As her barn grew, sadly her relationship with Derek deteriorated until they split up in 2017 after a 24-year relationship and more than a decade of marriage. It was a mutual separation but nonetheless difficult as there was so much to sort out in their messy divorce.

"It was devastating," says Laura. "As much as I wanted to pretend that I was coping, I had little motivation to carry on. I felt as if my whole world was crashing down around me – I'd lost my husband, a business partner and a good friend. I would go to my mum and dad's and all we would talk about was Derek and my house and what was going on with us sorting everything out in the divorce. My place was still filled with all of his stuff and I couldn't take the constant reminders of a marriage gone bad. So some nights I took a camp bed and I slept in the barn with the horses and my two dogs. Being close to the horses was very grounding for me. It was the only time I ever slept properly and I found a deep sense of peace there."

When Laura was feeling tearful and upset, she would stand with Angel and rest her head on hers. "She could sometimes have a wicked attitude if she didn't want to do something," says Laura, "but she could also be the softest, sweetest girl. The feel of her breath on my face was so comforting and reassuring to me because I knew that, no matter what, she was mine and nothing could ever change that. Angel would snuggle her face so close to mine while I cried and that was her way of letting me know that everything was going to be okay. She had a radar that told her when I was feeling sad and being in her presence was often enough to cheer me up."

After her divorce, Laura was lonely, and her friend Tracey decided that she needed to get out again and start dating. The trouble was, it had been so long since Laura had been in that world, she had no idea what to do. In 2018, about six months after her divorce, she met a guy called Freddie through Tracey. At 41 years old, Freddie, who came from Colombia, was the same age as Laura and was separated from his young son's mother. Over a coffee in Starbucks, Laura learned that they had a lot in common. Freddie, who lived in Orlando, had grown up around horses in his native country and he missed them terribly. He had always felt a connection with the animals, so Laura invited him to meet hers.

Soon, they were spending many hours together at the barn around the horses. Friends and family who saw them frequently commented that they were a match made in heaven, and they soon realized that they were in love.

In November 2018, they married in a beautiful ceremony at her parents' house next to the barn. Neither wanted to wait to date more. They were at the age where they didn't want to waste any time because they were so sure of their love for each other.

Together, along with Laura's parents, they run Dark Horse in between their day jobs. They have 11 horses of their own, all rescues who they have nursed back to health, and they now also have boarders who keep their horses at the barn and take lessons. It's hard work but they are a great team.

Laura says that if it wasn't for Angel her life would be so different now. Her horse was the one who inspired her and changed everything so much for the better.

"Angel is my soul horse," says Laura. "She is as much a part of me as I am of her. From the very first time I saw her in the stall, a quiet, withdrawn shadow of herself, I knew that we were going to be together. Over the years, she has helped me through so many situations that I know, if it hadn't been for her, I would never have got through those times. When I felt like giving up because I was humiliated by ignorant people at the horse shows, or sad at losing my husband, I only had to look at her and feel her face against mine. She gave me the heart to pull myself together. I know that I adopted her, but she has given me so much in return. I can't even think of a day when she's not in my life – she's twenty-three years old now and still living a fabulous, active existence. Angel is different to my other horses. She gives off an aura, as Freddie calls it. I call it an intense energy that I only feel when I'm around her. If I hadn't adopted her, I wouldn't have my barn or Freddie – I believe she has made all this happen. I'm blessed beyond measure that we found each other – she is such a special mare."

Chapter 23

ANGELA AND CAPONE THE DOG

As soon as Angela spotted the stray dog at the side of the busy road in Des Moines, Iowa, she pulled over in her car. It was trying to cross the road and seemed to be all alone beside the very busy Interstate 235 that runs through the city. Angela was concerned that if he ran into traffic, he would get hurt or, worse, killed.

The poor little black dog was incredibly thin with matted hair, but seemed friendly enough. He came right over to her, as if he wanted to be helped, so she bundled him into the car and went straight to her vet.

Angela had a deep love for dogs that started when she volunteered at her local animal-rescue charity when she was a teenager. If ever a dog or any other animal needed rescuing and Angela could help, she was the first one to step up, so when she saw the stray dog she had no hesitation in taking him in.

Her vet said that it was likely the pup had been on the streets for a long time since he was so painfully thin. There was no microchip that could be used to find his owner, so Angela took him home rather than him going to the dog pound with all the other strays. She contacted all her local rescue centres to see if anybody had reported the dog missing, but her detective work came up with nothing.

"I tried everything to find his family," says Angela. "He was such a super sweet little guy, a little nervous when I got him home but then very friendly, and I couldn't believe anyone would have let him go on purpose. When I couldn't find his owners, we decided to keep him. That is me, my husband Isaac – a large-truck driver – and our eight kids! They fell in love with him as soon as I brought him home – and, besides, there was no way I was going to take him to the dog pound. I knew we could give him a good home, so he stayed. It was one of the best decisions we have ever made."

The family named the scruffy little pup Capone, but they were still confused as to what breed he was – he looked like any one of a few. A DNA test showed that he is a miniature pinscher crossed with a chihuahua and a whippet. An interesting mix but, regardless, Capone was good-natured, kind and very loving.

Once Capone, who was thought to be about a year old, settled down with all the kids, he would play with them for hours and was very good with them. He became a big part of the family, and for a pretty small guy he was loud. Capone played hard, as if he had only just learned what fun really was, and it was soon apparent that he loved his new life with his adoptive family.

Isaac was often away truck-driving for several days at a time, and he always felt more comfortable about going after they got Capone. Isaac knew that the mightily protective Capone, even though he was a smaller dog, would look after his family in his absence – his pet gave him peace of mind when leaving them.

At around 1.30 a.m. in the early hours of 15 March 2017, Angela was asleep on the sofa after finally getting her six-month-old baby Atreu to sleep. He had been very fussy that night, so she had gone downstairs into the living room to avoid waking the other children. Isaac was away with work, so she was on her own again with the kids. Angela had just got to sleep when Capone started barking. "Please be quiet," she told him. "Don't you dare wake the baby up!"

Uncharacteristically, Capone ignored Angela and kept jumping up and barking. He wouldn't stop until she got up off the couch and followed him into the kitchen. As soon as Angela walked in, she saw a small fire in the alcove behind the microwave and there was smoke everywhere.

"Capone is usually very obedient and he certainly doesn't bark a lot," says Angela. "Particularly not in the night, anyway. I was so tired. The baby had been keeping me up every night and all I wanted to do was sleep, so when he kept disturbing me, I was a bit irritated at first in case he woke Atreu up. But the way he continued jumping up at me and barking wasn't like him, so I knew something was wrong. When I saw the fire, it was tiny and I thought I could put it out."

Angela called her dad Kent to see how to put out the fire, which seemed to be coming from the plug at the back of the microwave. Seconds later, the fire erupted into an inferno. Angela put the phone down and she knew that she had to get the kids out of the house as quickly as possible.

It was terrifying and it all happened so quickly. She got the older kids up first and they helped her to wake up their younger siblings, get them downstairs and out of the house. After a mad dash, everyone was out in the garden and Angela counted heads several times to make sure that all her children were there and that they were okay. Then she called the emergency services – by this time, the whole house was on fire.

It had taken just five minutes for the house to go up and thankfully everyone – including Capone, who never left Angela's side – was out and safe. A fire department investigation confirmed that it was bad electrics that had caused the fire to start in the plug socket behind the microwave.

The family lost everything. Thanks to the kindness of friends, family and strangers, who donated so much, they lived in hotels and then an apartment for six months while they rebuilt their lives. They eventually moved into another house and started all over again. It was an awful, difficult time. Everything that meant something to every single member of the family was gone – except for Capone, and everyone was so thankful he had escaped unharmed.

"I remember looking through the ashes for anything we could retrieve but there was nothing – the fire burned everything," says Angela. "We were so lucky that we made it out of there alive and we didn't get burned or hurt. If it hadn't been for Capone, it would have been a very different story. He saved his family that night. I'm so glad I listened to him because who knows what might have happened – it doesn't bear thinking about."

Capone's story hit the local news and he ended up winning a coveted medal from the Iowa Veterinary Medical Association and being inducted into the Iowa hall of fame for his heroism. He was also nominated for an American Humane Hero Dog award and his story has been shared all over the world as the rescue dog who literally rescued his owners right back.

"I am so thankful that we gave Capone a chance that day I spotted him at the side of the road," says Angela. "We couldn't have asked for a better dog who fitted in with our large family. He has repaid us in so many ways. That night, he was probably barking for a good two minutes before I woke up properly and realized that he was trying to tell me something, but he kept on until I listened. My kids and I were safe that night because of Capone. He is a dog in a million and he means the world to us. We will take care of him forever because he deserves that and more for saving our lives."

Chapter 24

HESTHER AND BLACK THE DONKEY

Ever since she can remember, Hesther had a fascination with the region around the Zambezi River in Zambia in south-eastern Africa. Her godparents were expats who lived there for many years before they returned to the UK, and her childhood was filled with their stories of life in a very different place. She loved to hear about the wild animals, the warm-hearted people and the countryside. Everything about the Zambezi sounded so colourful and exciting that she vowed to visit one day. That day came during her gap year between high school and university when Hesther, then 18, spent a year there as an au pair for an English family and a volunteer with a horse charity. The successful trip was enough to get Hesther completely hooked on the area and even when she returned to the UK, she spent her holidays in Zambia and never lost her deep affection for the Zambezi region.

She eventually landed the job of her dreams as a senior career advisor with a global company, helping international students gain places at universities in the UK and America. The area of the world that she covered was Africa, so this meant regular trips abroad. She managed to spend a lot of time in the Zambezi area of Zambia, making friends and subconsciously putting down roots.

"I know Zambezi isn't one of the best-known places in Africa but, for me, it quickly became the most special," says Hesther. "I fell in love with the raw beauty of the place – the countryside is so wild and unspoiled. The Zambezi people are genuine, kind and sweet despite the extreme poverty that exists. For the most part, it is a safe place with the most amazing animals wherever you look, and the sun is always shining brightly. I just knew deep down that one day I would leave the UK and live there. It was just a case of when and how I was going to do it. I feel that it was always written in my future."

In 2015, Hesther was part of a team that walked 250 miles across the Zambezi region to raise money to pay for new classrooms and much-needed schoolbooks for people living in a remote area. The hike was successful and an impressive £20,000 was generated for the cause. Along the way, Hesther discovered the heartbreaking truth about the plight of donkeys in Africa.

Donkeys are cheaper to buy than cattle in Africa, so many farmers use them to pull a cart on rough and rocky roads to take them to market many miles away. The farmers use a hardwood yoke designed for oxen and this makes the load heavy before the owner fills the cart with boxes of fruit, vegetables, baked goods and people. The yoke can give the donkeys bad sores that often go untreated and are left to fester. On immature animals, this can lead to severe deformation of the back and neck because, given their small stature, they are not suited to using such yokes. Once at the busy market, the donkeys are left out in the searing heat, covered in flies, and they are often not fed or given water while they wait. This is after they have usually walked miles to get there. The poor animals are then expected to make the trip home again at the end of the day, even though they are so exhausted that they can barely stand. It is a sad and pitiful existence in which the donkeys are regarded as vessels, not animals that deserve to be treated and valued much better.

On the long walk, Hesther saw many donkeys in bad shape, with gaping wounds, sore backs and what looked like long, painful hooves in need of trimming. The animals were having the life sucked out of them – and it devastated her. She couldn't stop thinking about the horrors she had seen, and they haunted her dreams. As soon as she returned to England, she made up her mind that she wanted to help the donkeys.

It was difficult doing so from the UK, however, but she spoke with friends and the seeds of a plan were sown while she also worked out a way of moving to Zambia permanently. She knew that the only serious way she could help them was to be based in the Zambezi region, where she could face the issues head-on, come up with solutions and be on hand to make them work.

"I realized that, although there are cruel owners, the vast majority of people who had donkeys lacked the basic knowledge needed to care for them properly," says Hesther. "Donkeys are very misunderstood – in Africa they are considered to be stubborn or stupid, so if they don't obey their owner, they are beaten until they submit and do as they are told. They are also worked until they drop, break their legs or die – even the poor pregnant donkeys are expected to work just as hard despite carrying their precious loads. It's an awful life for them and one of sheer torture. Once a donkey is unable to work any more, they are sold for cheap meat or to the donkey skins trade, which is emerging in Zambia's southern provinces, along the Zambezi. I cried at some of the scenes I witnessed, and I knew that I had to do something about those poor, defenceless creatures. It was just a question of the right timing."

It wasn't until Hesther got divorced from her husband that she was finally able to put into action her moving plans. She was in Africa several times a year with her job, so she persuaded her boss to let her live there permanently.

In 2017, she moved to Zambia and it was like she was finally going home. Not long after, she met her current partner Tom at a friend's barbecue. He just so happened to be a huge animal lover like Hesther, and he helped her to start up the Zambezi Working Donkey Project (ZWDP) in 2019. The first donkey they helped in July of that same year is one who will forever be in Hesther's heart for many different reasons.

It took the team three months to get custody of Black because her owner didn't want to give her up. She was eventually brought to the ZWDP's mobile veterinary care clinic in the remote Kasiya village out in the bush with a hoof that was almost hanging off. The poor girl was in agony from the injury, which had been caused by her being tied up with wire that became embedded in her leg. She couldn't even feed her foal because she was in so much pain, and by the time Hesther got Black and the baby back to her ranch for treatment, she didn't know if they would survive.

Seeing a donkey in such a bad state was heart-rending and Hesther shed many tears over the unfairness of it all. It was difficult to understand how anyone could treat an animal so appallingly. The stress of this first rescue led to sleepless nights about whether or not Black could be saved, yet – by nothing short of a miracle – she lived, and so did her foal, who the project aptly named Future.

It was during the difficult times that Hesther gained a great deal of comfort from the very soul she was helping to save – darling Black. Her healing was a slow and steady process, but the way Black would nuzzle Hesther so gently, as if she were saying thank you, gave Hesther the drive to carry on as the project helped more donkeys.

"When I first met Black, I cried a lot," recalls Hesther. "She was in such an awful state. She couldn't walk and she was in a lot of pain. She was weak and couldn't feed her baby, which was awful to see, so we were dealing with not just one but two very sick donkeys. Seeing an animal suffer is horrific and it played on my mind a lot. There were times when it felt that the job was too difficult, that we could never win, but just being around Black and Future and knowing the difference we made to their lives spurred me on. I quickly realized that crying wasn't going to get anything done. Black definitely gave me strength on the more difficult days and at times of crisis to keep calm and to carry on. Looking at her with her foal in the field was an absolute joy and they gave me a renewed sense of purpose. Black made it clear that she was grateful for our help with her sweet nuzzles and the way she would bray when she saw me. No matter how awful I felt inside, she would make me smile and pick myself up. I owe her so much."

Black, who walks with a limp, now lives a very nice life and she will never have to work again. Future, who grew strong, was adopted by a new family and he also lives a good life – they are one of the project's greatest success stories.

The project has been busy since 2019. Hesther and her volunteers set up an outreach programme visiting rural villages and life has already significantly improved for many donkeys. The project advises owners on how to care for their animals and how to treat them with the respect that they deserve. The team also provides new cart harnesses that are lighter and fit the donkeys much better, therefore avoiding injuries. Hesther and her team also care for donkeys with all different kinds of wounds. They treat skin parasites and worms, and they teach owners about foot and hoof care. The locals are usually interested and keen to learn, which is a good start.

By the beginning of 2021, the project has checked and nursed more than 740 donkeys and provided new harnesses for 230 carts. They have aided more than 250 owners from over 80 different villages, and the hard work continues.

Every day, Hesther gains from the donkeys her inspiration and her determination to help make a world where they are free from pain and suffering, and where they are valued by the people who rely on them. There are success stories and some not so good days, as with any animal rescue. The project recently lost its first donkey – an orphaned foal who had been found wandering around a village all alone. Despite being bottle-fed, he was too weak to survive. His death was devastating and difficult to accept, but it only made the project's work even more important.

Hesther has around 13 donkeys that live at her farm but, for the most part, she tries to reunite any she rescues with their owners, providing it is safe to do so, or find new homes for them. It is her life's mission, and she wouldn't want to be anywhere else.

"Donkeys are such endearing characters," says Hesther. "They put up with so much. They can be in extreme pain, but you would never know it because they are resilient creatures. Often you wouldn't be aware that they are sick until they literally fall to their knees. These animals are so smart and nothing is more rewarding for me than cuddling and loving on a donkey we have rescued. You can feel the affection and appreciation, and this closeness makes everything so worthwhile. I've had days when I've seen such cruelty that it makes me feel sick and, honestly, quite depressed. But then I only have to go in the field and be with the donkeys and they pick me up in a way no one else can.

"I learned that being an emotional mess every time I found an abused donkey wouldn't do me or the project any good," Hesther concludes. "They have taught me to be strong and practical for them and myself. There are too many donkeys to count who need our help. It's going to take years to change deep-rooted perceptions of donkeys in Africa, but we are willing to fight for every single one of them. Black will always be my first love. She has shown me what resilience against adversity really is. Seeing her thrive means everything and I will be forever grateful our paths crossed."

Chapter 25

ANNIE AND CHERRY THE HORSE

Without warning, Annie's health began to deteriorate dramatically. At first, she just felt tired all the time and was convinced that it was her body's reaction to a stressful year.

As the weeks went by, the tiredness turned into chronic fatigue; some days she couldn't even get out of bed and, if she did, the exertion would make her physically sick. Her hair started to fall out. Initially it was the odd strand, but then it came out in clumps. The tips of her fingers would split and bleed for no reason and it was very distressing.

Annie, a former international athlete who competed in cross-country and the 3,000-m race for Great Britain, was terrified that she was dying. Over the course of a year, she saw many doctors who, despite a barrage of tests, couldn't come up with a diagnosis. It was frustrating and scary. Annie wanted answers and she would feel worse every day that passed by, despite her doctors' reassurances that, while she was very ill, she wasn't dying.

"I had been so physically fit for years with my background as an athlete and then a personal trainer," says Annie. "I was completely unprepared for getting ill. I'd never been ill in my life. While I would lie in bed, my life flashed before me. I felt vulnerable, often alone and afraid of what was going to happen to me. I didn't understand why my doctors couldn't find answers. I remember thinking of all the things that I had wanted to do with my life but hadn't got around to. They included learning to ride and owning a horse. I wondered, had I left it too late to fulfil my dream? Had I left a lot of things too late? I was still only in my early thirties and I was young. I always thought I had the time, but then I wasn't so sure. It was a very sobering thought."

Eventually, Annie was referred to an endocrinologist and he finally had the answers she was so desperately searching for. She was diagnosed with an autoimmune condition called Hashimoto's disease. It's a relatively rare condition where the immune system attacks the thyroid and damages it so that it can't make enough hormones. There is no cure, but it can be treated. Annie's doctor told her that it would take about a year for the medicine to start working properly because it is such a complex disease, so she would have to be patient. While Annie did start to feel a little better, the wait was excruciating, and her anxiety levels heightened. Every day was difficult – if not physically, then emotionally, as she wondered if she would ever feel properly well again.

During this trying time, she decided to make good on her promise to herself to start horse riding and buy a horse. A friend of hers had rescued a beautiful dark bay thoroughbred mare from an auction three years before. While no longer with the friend, the horse, Cherry, who was very flighty and uncontrollable, and had come from a racing yard very thin and unhealthy after giving birth to a foal, might again be available.

Cherry had been very stressed at the market and no one had bid on her, which meant that she was going to be sold for meat. It's a sad fact that at horse auctions in the UK, animals are often sold to the meat trade. Annie's friend hadn't been able to bear the idea of the mare going to the slaughterhouse, so had persuaded the auctioneer to let her take the horse for a small adoption fee, far less than the meat men would have paid for her. She had taken her home, but Cherry had been difficult to train, so she'd sold her to another young woman who struggled with her, too. Cherry was a stunning-looking horse, but she was considered to be dangerous and untrainable by her new owner.

When Annie heard about Cherry and her sad background, she jumped at the chance to have her. Nobody else wanted her and Annie was afraid that the mare would end up in the wrong hands. Despite not knowing much about horses, Annie took her home in November 2013.

"It sounds a bit impulsive but, as soon as I found out about Cherry, I wanted her," recalls Annie. "She had such a sad backstory and I wanted to give her a chance. She was just in the wrong hands. The girl who had her wanted a quick fix and she had thought that she could train her, but Cherry needed time, love and a lot of attention. And even though I knew that she was too much horse for me, I fell in love with her face and her deep, beautiful eyes that hid her former life of misery at the racing stables. Cherry was a very stressed-out animal, the type of mare who thinks everything that's not in her routine is a big deal. What she needed was someone confident to guide her and show her the way."

While Annie was still not in the best of health and prone to relapses, when she would be exhausted and bedridden for days, she visited her horse as much as she could. Cherry had a reputation at her new livery yard as being a troublesome mare who kicked out and hurt people, so Annie made sure that she was there every morning and evening to take care of her.

The following January, tragedy struck. Cherry broke the splint bone in her leg after an accident in the field, and while everyone told Annie to put the mare to sleep because the recovery was lengthy and complex, she couldn't do it. It took £8,000 and two surgeries, but Cherry survived. It was a long, difficult year before she was in a rideable condition again, but during that time Annie and Cherry bonded in the most beautiful way.

"While my health was still dodgy, Cherry needed me more than anyone," says Annie. "My desire to see her was stronger than my tiredness. I may have been very ill some days, but I didn't let it beat me. Being around Cherry was comforting and peaceful. I would sit talking to her for ages in the stable, willing her to get better, and she would listen to me. I know that she recovered not just for herself but for me, too. The more time I spent with her, the better my anxiety seemed to get, and the less stressed-out Cherry was. We were a good influence on each other and while she grew healthier and stronger, so did I. When I was with Cherry, I felt that anything was possible. There was something so spiritual about her; she was more than a horse – she was a soulmate and I know that she felt that level of connection with me, too."

Eventually, Annie was able to ride Cherry for the first time and they would spend hours in the streets and in local fields. Annie knew that if she was anxious, it would filter through to Annie, so she learned to control her worries while they were together.

Sadly, in March 2018, Cherry fell sick with colic, which wouldn't go away. Her vet discovered a massive blockage in her large intestine and there was nothing that he could do to save her. As Cherry lay with her head in Annie's hands, Annie talked to her softly through her tears. "I am so grateful to you, my Cherry," she told her. "Everyone is going to know your name. You will never be forgotten."

It was one of the most traumatic experiences that Annie had ever lived through, but she had to give Cherry one of her most precious gifts as an owner – the gift of not letting her pass away all alone. For Annie, it was so important that she was with her girl when she died.

After Cherry passed away, Annie felt lost. Not long after, on a mercy trip to Cernavodă in Romania to help save stray dogs, she became aware of the thousands of horses who were on the roads. In Romania, horses are considered to be nothing more than machines. It's the way of life in a poor country where horses are used to pull carts or ploughs and to carry people. The majority that Annie saw were so skinny they looked like they would pass out. Their hooves were long and untrimmed, some were crippled, their teeth had never been looked after, and others had open sores where they had just been neglected. It was an awful situation and Annie decided that she needed to do something to help – in Cherry's name.

In late 2018, she set up Cherry Horse Welfare International, which focuses its efforts on helping horses in Romania; there is now also a UK branch that deals with the overbreeding of thoroughbreds. Volunteers work with other charities in an area to provide education and supplies to horse owners, such as rugs for the winter months, bridles that fit and head collars. It is much-needed assistance and many horses have benefitted from donations and the work of the charity.

"I don't judge or blame the owners for the state of their animals," says Annie. "In Romania, they live a very tough life and this is all many of them have ever known. It is a poor country and there are definitely some cruelty cases, but a lot of what goes on is because, unfortunately, the people don't know any better and they don't have the resources. I made a promise to Cherry on her deathbed that in her memory

I would do everything I could to help the plight of other horses and this was the perfect opportunity for me to honour her name. We've since set up an outreach facility where people can bring their horses to get their hooves trimmed, teeth rasped and have a general health check. This makes such a difference to the lives of the horses."

Cherry will always hold a very special space in Annie's heart. While she may have rescued the mare, her actions were reciprocated and their bond will never go away.

"I hold Cherry in my soul," says Annie. "She may not be here in the physical world but she's always with me. We had a bond like none I've ever felt before. We had so many hours of fun. She was my best friend and she made me a much better person. I think that she felt secure and loved because we had a mutual trust. I'm not sure I will experience that kind of love again. She was such a special horse."

Chapter 26

TIFFANY AND ANGEL THE DOG

Alexandra's favourite type of dog had always been the pit bull. She adored them, partly because people gave the breed such grief for being aggressive and dangerous. In many countries they are banned as pets, and she saw that in her local Texas shelters there were always many more pit bulls that needed rescuing than other dogs.

Alexandra felt that she could relate to the plight of the breed, which she long thought was misunderstood, like she was. At just 4 feet 10 inches tall and 98 lb, she was tiny. When she was a teenager, she was constantly getting taken advantage of in her relationships with boys and even by some of her girlfriends. She developed a tough exterior that masked her heart of gold. It was easier than getting walked all over by people and getting hurt.

When she was old enough to have her own place, she adopted pit bulls from the shelter, and it was her animals who always helped her through the tough times in her love life.

"My daughter was one of a kind with the biggest heart for animals, particularly those in need," says Alexandra's mom Tiffany. "She was always attracted to the underdog and her pets were more like her babies, she loved them so much. I always remember her telling me how much the dogs helped her when she was going through tough times. The way they would lick her face, follow her around the house and never leave her side. She always said that she was the lucky one, not them, that they had found each other."

It's fair to say that Alexandra had her fair share of ups and downs. She left school early, met a young man and quickly fell pregnant with their son Colin, who was born in July 2009. The relationship with his father didn't last, so she adapted to life as a single parent. To make ends meet, she took a job as an exotic dancer in a local club. The money was good and, being the fiercely independent young woman she was, it meant that she could look after Colin and that he never wanted for anything.

One night, she danced for a man at the club and he asked her out on a date. Alexandra typically did not date her clients from the bar, but this one seemed different. He was tall and handsome, and they hit it off. She dated the guy, Danny Munguia, on and off for a few months. She also met another man, Gilbert, in 2011 and she dated him, too. Tiffany says that her daughter didn't want to be tied down or settle for just one person – she was waiting for Mr Right to come along. She had a romantic notion that someone would turn up and save her.

After a year-and-a-half relationship, Gilbert moved away to Corpus Christi, another part of Texas. Heartbroken, Alexandra immediately took up with Danny again, who was only too happy to step in. This time, she fell head over heels in love with Danny, but their relationship was toxic. One night, in January 2013, Tiffany was called to the hospital because Danny had headbutted Alexandra in the forehead.

"I remember there was blood everywhere and she had a massive gash that needed seventeen stiches," recalls Tiffany. "It was horrible. She told me that they had fought over money or something and he lost control. She reported the incident to the police, and I took her home with me. I asked her and Colin to stay with me because it wasn't safe for them to be living with Danny. Two weeks later, after he had begged her for forgiveness and promised her the world, she gave in and went back to him. She loved him and she decided that, despite his temper, life was ultimately better with him in it. I pleaded with her not to go. I told her it was a big mistake – I was a victim of domestic violence and I knew that an abuser rarely changed, no matter how hard they promise that they will. Alexandra told me that she couldn't be apart from him any longer. She said that their relationship was full of passion and that sometimes it got out of control. I guess that was one way of defending him."

Not long after, clearly unhappy because the abuse was continuing, Alexandra jumped at the chance to move to Corpus Christi with Gilbert. She became pregnant but they fell out again and Danny brought her home. He promised he would change, and he agreed to take on her unborn child as his own. When baby Adelina was born in January 2014, he was every bit the proud dad and he gave her his last name.

Sadly, their happiness was short-lived. They were struggling to pay their bills and they had endless rows about money. Danny, who worked as a pipe-fitter in an oil field, wouldn't let Alexandra get a job and she was lonely at home. She wanted to earn her own money so that, if they ever split up, she was in a good financial position to make it again by herself. Alexandra knew in her heart that one day she would leave him.

The only way she got through the extreme rows and unhappiness was thanks to her rescue dogs, and one in particular, Angel. Alexandra had found Angel, a red pit bull, on Facebook in December 2013. She had been rescued from a breeder who had treated her appallingly. She had given birth to countless puppies and was kept chained up outside with little food and no love. Alexandra already had her two pit-bull rescues, but when she saw the pictures of Angel, she wanted to help. She contacted the lady, Diane, who had taken Angel in, and without even seeing her, Alexandra offered to give her a permanent home.

As soon as she met Angel, it was instant love. While the dog wouldn't let anyone else get close to her, she allowed Alexandra to get into the cage with her and Angel crawled into her lap. The poor girl was skin and bone, and Diane said that Alexandra must be the chosen one.

Angel flourished with Alexandra and her two adopted siblings. She loved everyone except for Danny – she wouldn't let him go near her and she was extremely protective of Alexandra, particularly when he was around. During their frequent arguments, Angel would bark and snarl at Danny, and Alexandra told Tiffany that he would lock the dogs outside at these times because he knew that they would bite him if he tried to hurt her. That was the only way he managed to beat her.

When Danny was at work, Alexandra and Angel were inseparable. She provided much-needed comfort with her sweet puppy-dog kisses, and Alexandra relied on her to get her through the bad days, of which there were many.

As the months went by, her relationship with Danny deteriorated further. In her diary in May 2014, she wrote: "I feel like I have to hide in my own house. I keep asking myself is the love worth my life."

Sadly, on 4 July 2014, Alexandra was found dead at her home. Danny called the police and said that they had had a row the night before over money and jobs, and he had found her lying face down in the living room in a pool of blood.

The truth was that Danny had beaten her around the head with a piece of granite and had also strangled her. She hadn't stood a chance against him. The dogs had been locked out at the time so they couldn't save her. Years later, in January

2020, Danny finally pleaded guilty to her murder and a judge sentenced him to life in prison for his crime.

After Tiffany heard the news of her daughter's death, she went straight to Alexandra's house and took Angel home while friends took the other two dogs.

"I never thought that Danny would really hurt Alexandra, but I underestimated him," says Tiffany. "Losing her was the most devastating thing I've ever experienced. It felt like my soul had been torn in two. I couldn't believe how anyone who said that they loved someone as much as he did could do something so evil. To make matters worse, we later found out that he murdered Alexandra in front of the baby. I remember I went to the house and there was Angel in the back garden. I could tell that she knew that something was wrong because she was just sitting there alone and she looked so sad. Luckily, she knew me well and came right over. I threw my arms around her and we cried hard together. I swear I saw tears rolling down her face – it was just so heartbreaking. I had to take her home with me because she was a connection to my daughter and I know it's what Alexandra would have wanted."

Tiffany also took custody of Adelina and has since adopted her. Poor Angel struggled to come to terms with losing her mom, just as Tiffany mourned the loss of her daughter, and they bonded over their intense, gut-wrenching grief. When Tiffany needed time alone, though she was the rock who held the family together in the weeks and months after Alexandra's murder, Angel wouldn't hear of it. She would follow Tiffany around the house and sit as close as she could while Tiffany let her tears flow. Angel would look at her in a certain gut-wrenching way and Tiffany would say sadly, "I know," and they would hug each other hard. When Tiffany saw tears in dear Angel's eyes, she would gently wipe them away and tell her, "It's okay, Angel, we love you, too," and the dog would rest her head in Tiffany's lap until the moment subsided.

"We made a big fuss of Angel," recalls Tiffany. "We kept some of Alexandra's clothes and she slept with them. I noticed that, when she was really missing her, she would snuggle with those shirts. It must have been the comfort of her scent. Other times, she would come to me. It was the saddest thing I've ever seen. While I had lost my beautiful girl, she had lost the one person she trusted and loved most in the world. After suffering a living hell with her previous owner, she had finally found happiness and it had been cruelly taken away from her. While there were times when I wanted to give in to my grief, I couldn't because I had Adelina and Angel to take care of. They gave me purpose because they both needed me more than ever. They needed someone who was strong, and I had to be that person. Of course, I cried a lot and, in those moments, Angel was the one who was strong. We helped each other because we understood what we were both going through like no one else really could."

Almost two years after Alexandra was murdered, Angel passed away suddenly. Tiffany found her one morning in her bed snuggled next to her mom's shirt. She had died from natural causes, but Tiffany still believes it was because of a broken heart. Losing Angel was tough, but Tiffany firmly believes that Alexandra was waiting for her when she passed and that the two of them have been reunited in a much happier place, both free of pain and sadness.

While the house is still quiet without Angel, the family will never forget the rescued pup who, in her own grief, managed to keep them smiling and who gave them the will to carry on when it seemed impossible.

"Angel and I, well, we rescued each other," says Tiffany. "Unfortunately, I was never going to mend her broken heart, but we did at least have two wonderful years together when she meant so much to me. She wasn't just a link to Alexandra – she was my friend and I loved her so much. It was rough when she passed over and I cried for days. It was so damn still in our house without her presence. However, some of those were happy tears because I knew she had been reunited with the love of her life, Alexandra, and that was such a good thing. I will be forever grateful to Angel for the love that she showed me and my family. I like to think that she and Alexandra are watching over me and Adelina – I feel their presence sometimes. Angel definitely lived up to her name – she was my angel here on earth and I will always have her in my heart."

Chapter 27

NICKY AND SPARE THE CAT

It really was very strange. Nicky's two cats Storm and Hex weren't getting any fatter, yet the big bowl of food that was left in the kitchen for them at night was empty every morning. Nicky and her husband David lived in a ground-floor flat in east London, and each night they left the back door, which was protected by iron bars, open so the cats could roam around.

In order to solve the mystery, David, who works in computers, set up a webcam in the kitchen to find out where all their cats' rather expensive food was disappearing to. The next morning, the mystery was solved.

The pair watched as an enormous black and white cat stole in through the bars. It was very odd-looking, with stumpy little legs, severely matted hair and half a tail.

"It was obviously a feral cat," says Nicky. "It was pretty ugly, like it was made up of lots of spare parts that had been sewn together. We watched as it sneaked in and ate all the food, then disappeared again into the night. Although my husband David was a bit annoyed that this probably flea-infested cat was taking food, we decided to leave it be. For the next year or so, the cat kept appearing. Storm, who was sociable with humans and other cats, took a shine to him. He would bring the stray home with him sometimes, who would then go off again on his own."

In February 2015, a massive storm battered England. The severe winds rattled windows and blew off gutters, hail smashed to the ground and onto roofs, and the rain was torrential. Nicky had Storm and Hex safely inside, but that evening, as they were hunkered down in the living room watching TV, the stray cat staggered into the room and slithered under the sofa. He appeared so bedraggled and ill that Nicky wondered if he had come into the house to die. Although he let her look at him, he refused to be touched and cried softly when she went near him.

Nicky locked the cat alone in the living room and called the Celia Hammond Animal Trust, a charity for cats. They sent one of their volunteers over to pick him up and, even though he was so ill, he put up one heck of a fight and tore up the kitchen and some curtains. Later, a staff member from Celia Hammond called Nicky to update her on the cat and it was a sad story. Their vet estimated that the cat was at least 15 to 20 years old, his teeth were rotting to the bone and he had a urinary tract infection and a serious virus. It was a miracle he was still alive but Nicky was warned that, even if he did pull through, he might only have six months to a year to live because he was so old and in such bad shape. Part of the deal that the charity would have him neutered, extract his rotting teeth, give him his inoculations and nurse him back to health was that Nicky had to agree to let him live in her garden and to keep feeding him. She did so, of course. Cats were a huge part of her life and she wanted to help this stray cat, even though she didn't really know him. What she did know was that there was something so endearing about him and that she could help him. As he was feral, she was advised to let him stay outside and come indoors for his food because he would never change – being out alone in the world was all that he knew.

In April, the cat was returned to them and they named him Spare – as in the couple's spare cat. He needed to recuperate for another two weeks, so Nicky put him in the spare bedroom and hoped for the best. When he was better, she let him out and he went missing for three weeks. Nicky was beside herself until she and David spotted him nearby around some bins. She put down some food and that night he returned, much to her relief.

In November 2015, Nicky and David moved into a new house. They took all three cats with them – there was no way they were leaving Spare behind – and for several weeks he again stayed in the spare room. This time, Nicky went in to see him every day. She read him stories from books and gently nudged tuna underneath the bed where he hid out. He came out for food – usually when she had gone – but she persevered.

"Spare was such a character," says Nicky. "He was a typical feral cat. He didn't want anything to do with us humans – I just don't think that he trusted us even when we gave him food. He could have been on the streets all his life for all we knew, but when we moved there was no way I was leaving him behind to fend for himself again. I'd got used to him being around and we had made a promise to him when he got better that we would look after him. It was peaceful sitting with him. I would perch on cushions on the floor a few feet away from the bed and read to him, in the hope he would get used to my voice and to humans in general. I wanted him to learn to trust me and to be happy in his final months. It was very important to me and to David to provide that security for Spare."

In March 2016, Nicky experienced a devastating loss when she suffered a miscarriage at eight weeks into her pregnancy. At the time, she and David were attending a funeral and she was rushed to the hospital. It was the month before her marriage to David and the night before her hen party. It was an awful loss and a huge shock for the couple, who were keen to have a family. After being given the horrible news, Nicky went home and to bed to grieve her lost child. The next day, she woke up and, to her surprise, Spare was sitting right on the end of her bed and was staring at her intently.

Up until this time, he hadn't let her touch or stroke him, and he had never come into her bedroom. In fact, he had spent all of his time outdoors, only coming in for his dinner at night and to use the spare room.

"I couldn't believe my eyes," says Nicky. "There he was, that big old ball of hair who hadn't ever come near me or David, sat on my bed, watching me. I woke up feeling so lousy and sad. The miscarriage had been so unexpected and I was still in shock. I had cried so much that I almost had no more tears to cry. So when I saw Spare sat there, I almost couldn't believe it, and from then on he slept every single night at the end of the bed on my side. It only took a couple of days more until he inched closer and nuzzled me. This was the cat who, although he had never hurt me or David, would try to slap us with his paw if we went too close."

Nicky was soothed by Spare's presence: "Having such a distraction was very welcome in the early days after my miscarriage and a comfort because he would not leave the room if I was there. From then on, I would wake up in the morning with him pushing his nose under my arm and he would often sleep next to my back, as if he had to be close to me. I loved the feel of Spare's fur against me and I never felt alone because of him. I like to think that he sensed my grief and deep loss and he wanted to help. I looked into cat psychology and I read that when a cat sleeps close to you, he feels like he's part of the family. I am certain that's what happened with Spare and we bonded in a bigger way than I did with my other two."

David and Nicky were married in April 2016 and one of their wedding gifts was a little white female kitten. Spare loved the baby and showed a very paternal side. The kitten loved him, too, and they would play together.

In April 2017, Nicky became pregnant again and this time everything went well, apart from terrible morning sickness that kept her housebound in the early days. Spare, who had taken on a new lease of life caring for the kitten, took it upon himself to bring Nicky special gifts of moist mice. Storm did the same and Nicky read that in the cat world this is a sign that they are looking after the pregnant mother.

On her days spent on the sofa feeling sick and watching Netflix, it was Spare who sat with her to keep her company. He would put his paws gently on her stomach as if he knew that there was a baby growing in there.

Interestingly, when Nicky's beautiful daughter Violet was born in December 2017, Spare became obsessed with her and they turned out to be the very best of friends. Violet's first word was, fittingly, "cat". When she learned to walk, Spare followed her around the house, rarely leaving her side. Violet was, quite simply, Spare's human. They played dress-up together, and she made him wear a crown, which he loved. Spare's favourite game was doctors and when he saw her pull out her toys, he purred loudly with excitement, much to Violet's amusement and happiness. The pair of them were a team and it was so touching to witness.

"Violet was his girl and he was very much her favourite," says Nicky. "If she cried, he ran over and nuzzled her. She talked to him all the time and he was the first thing she wanted to see when she got home from childcare. She shared her food with him. Wherever she was, he was, too, like a protective shadow. He showered her with such love and affection, and sometimes I couldn't believe this was the same feral cat who, before I had the miscarriage, didn't want anything to do with any of us."

After Violet was born, Nicky had two more miscarriages, including the loss of twins at ten weeks in January 2019. She was hospitalized and had a week at home after her surgery. Spare was there again, constantly by Nicky's side to offer much-needed comfort at another terribly difficult time. Spare was also a bright, shining light during the Covid-19 lockdowns.

"Covid gave Spare the perfect lifestyle," says Nicky. "He was so extremely happy to have us around all day and he followed us from room to room before he sat down next to me, unless he was playing with Violet. He purred constantly, or he grabbed your hand with both paws and put it on himself to be stroked. He was the cutest thing and a real tonic during the times we spent away from family and friends. I felt that this was his way of thanking us for saving him all those years ago. Even though he was very old, had lost the sight in one of his eyes and I knew he was tired, when he saw Violet, he still lit up. Spare was such a very special cat. In fact, he was a once-in-a-lifetime cat. He was such a gentle soul and we love him. I know there will never be another like him."

Sadly, in December 2020, after a long and eventful life, Spare passed away. Nicky scattered his ashes in the garden among the forget-me-nots.

Chapter 28

TRACEY AND SCOUT THE DOG

Tracey and her husband Paul had always loved the whippet breed of dog. Theirs, Misty, was such a kind, loving little animal – and because one whippet just isn't enough, they welcomed Isy into their home not long after. They thought their family was complete – and it was, until a chance conversation at the veterinary practice, where Tracey worked as a nurse, led to something amazing.

It was around March 2011 and Tracey overheard a discussion about a whippet–greyhound cross who needed adopting. As soon as she heard the word whippet, her ears pricked up. The pup, who was just a few months old, had been taken in off the streets of Durham, in the north of England, by a dog warden who had found him all alone, whimpering by the side of the road. It is thought that he had been on his own for quite a while because he was so thin, and he was in a bad way with matted fur and sore eyes. Once the vet he'd been seen by had examined him, he had been found to be partially blind, which would probably explain why he had been dumped by whoever had owned him. The poor boy also had kennel cough and mange, and the vet had thought he was deaf, too.

The pup had been put in isolation because of his cough while it was decided what to do with him. Yet his bad health hadn't dampened his enthusiasm for life, and he was friendly with everyone who met him. At first, the consensus had been to euthanize him because he was blind and deaf – it had been considered the more humane choice rather than letting him suffer. But then the vet, who just hadn't felt right about putting him to sleep at such an early age, had given him one last chance – he'd tapped the floor to see if the puppy heard anything at all. And he had! He had barked furiously as soon as he'd heard the noise so, with that in mind, he had got a reprieve.

Blind dogs are adopted all the time, so it was decided that he deserved a second chance. The puppy ended up at the East Midlands Dog Rescue, which is how Tracey's surgery heard about him. The surgery provided veterinary services for dogs who were taken in off the streets or surrendered by families.

"As soon as I heard about the puppy, I had to go and see him," says Tracey. "I'd thought about adopting a dog before, and when this one came along, I saw it as a sign. The pup was in a run with a lurcher when we got to the rescue centre and he came bounding over to see Paul and me. He almost missed us but we caught the scruffy little thing – he was very tatty, half bald, out of proportion and scabby. They weren't joking when they told us he was in a bad way. But there was such a joy in him! He was so excited to meet us, even though his vision was limited. It didn't stop him leaping all over us, so thrilled to have some attention. It was instant love and I told them right away we would take him. I was also afraid that no one else would want him with his disabilities and I knew that we could give him a good home with our other dogs."

After their initial meeting went so well, Tracey and Paul went back to the rescue centre with Misty and Isy just to make sure that they would get on okay with the puppy. The couple took them all for a walk and while the puppy kept on falling off the kerb and bouncing between them, not once were Misty and Isy mean to him. Instead, they stayed close, as if they were protecting him.

The successful introduction was enough for them to take him home to be with his new siblings. They called him Scout and quickly discovered quite how remarkable and resilient he was. Despite one of his eyes not forming properly and the other being affected by a genetic disease, he was quick to find his way around: as soon as he got in his new house, he mind-mapped each room by sniffing around the perimeter of the space so he could get an idea of what was there and where things were placed. It was quite brilliant to watch and, before long, he could go from room to room safely without crashing into the furniture. Tracey had to be extra tidy so that nothing was out of place otherwise it would throw Scout. She also kept all the doors open so he could move freely around the house.

She enrolled him in puppy-training classes, which he loved. Scout also liked nothing better than going for walks with Misty and Isy, and it was an amazing sight to see Misty herding him back to Tracey if he wandered too far away on his own.

Scout fitted right in with his new family and everyone adored his infectious zest for life. He may have had a rocky start and been blind, but his enthusiasm was an absolute joy to see.

In 2015, Tracey's dad, Alan, was diagnosed with liver cancer. The two were very close and his illness hit her really hard, particularly when it was found to have spread throughout his body. He was given just months to live. Tracey spent as much time as she could with him, and he loved to hear her tales of Scout and what he had been up to.

When Tracey got home, stressed and in tears, Scout would be waiting for her, so happy to see her and eager to lick her face and give her a lot of love. Scout had a knack of making her smile even when she felt so sad that she couldn't stop crying.

The night before Alan passed away, Tracey and Scout did their Bronze Award for the Good Citizen Dog Scheme, which is a UK Kennel Club test that aims to promote responsible dog ownership and enhance an owner's relationship with their dog. It is a series of examinations of the dog's basic training that includes walking to heel without pulling, being well behaved in crowds, allowing his owner to clean and groom him, and then standing for inspection by the judges.

Scout passed with flying colours. "The lady who passed us said it was the highlight of her day watching our Scout," recalls Tracey. "I was so proud of him. We had been practising while Dad had been ill, and it was such a welcome distraction from the upset of watching Dad deteriorate. As soon as we got the award, I thought about Dad and I knew how proud he would be. While he was sick, I would tell him what me and Scout had been doing and he loved to listen – Scout made him smile even on his worst days. In the months that followed his death, it was Scout who helped me deal with the intense grief I felt. He had an ability to know when I wasn't feeling myself and he wouldn't leave me. He would lick away my tears, which was such a comfort."

Scout was not only a godsend as Tracey navigated her grief, but he also helped her to come to terms with an event that happened long before he was even born.

Tracey's first dog was a whippet named Ruby. She was a quiet, timid little thing who was frightened of everything. Tracey walked her to get her used to being out of the house and her safe zone, and also to get her used to seeing other dogs. For a while it worked, until one fateful morning.

A terrier from around the corner appeared from nowhere and ran at Ruby, growling and barking. Tracey scooped Ruby up in her arms because her dog was panicking, but she stopped breathing and tragically died in Tracey's arms. Distraught, Tracey rushed her to the vets where she worked but they were unable to save her – she had suffered a massive heart attack. Her loss was unfathomable and Tracey felt guilty that, as a veterinary nurse, she hadn't been able to save her precious baby girl.

That feeling of guilt stayed with Tracey and when she got Misty and Isy her anxiety levels went through the roof whenever she walked them in case the same thing happened again. She became wary of walking them and she was always on the lookout to avoid other dogs. But when Scout arrived, everything had to change. Tracey had to find her confidence again and address her fear because Scout needed her to be his eyes, to guide him and to watch and make sure he didn't get hurt. With such a focus on keeping Scout safe, there was no room for excessive worry and Tracey found the challenges rewarding. While her fears are not completely cured, her anxiety is definitely better.

Scout is also making a difference in the lives of the residents in a dementia care home after he successfully passed his tests to become a therapy dog. He is a much-loved visitor to the residents, who look forward to seeing him.

"Most people love to pet him and give him attention," says Tracey. "He is so quiet and patient with them – for a few minutes he lights up their world. I remember there was one lady who didn't like being around other people and she would keep her room dark all the time – she seemed so sad, and it was heartbreaking. But she let me in with Scout and she told me that she was a farmer's wife who had had dogs all her life. She started to smile at her memories, and we had a lovely chat while she stroked Scout. He brought her out of her bubble and just for a little bit that sweet old dear was transported back to what were her happy times. I like to think that it was all Scout's doing."

Tracey and Scout were also invited to give a talk at a local community carers café event, where he provided emotional-support therapy to people with all sorts of problems, from depression and anxiety to other mental-health issues. He was so popular that they were asked to go back twice a month. Attendees couldn't get enough of Scout's cuddles – no matter what, he was always able to lift the mood in the room.

Sadly, Scout's genetic condition has worsened; although he is completely blind now, nothing stops him. And he inspires everyone he meets with his happy personality and love of life.

When Tracey's sister Donna had to have surgery to remove an eye, she woke up in hospital and said, "Do I look like Scout now?" She felt self-conscious because she had to wear a prosthetic. Tracey persuaded her to go for a walk in the park with Scout and then they stopped for afternoon tea in a café. Donna said having Scout was a boost because, far from people staring at her, they were looking at and fussing over him instead.

"Scout has made such an impact on the lives of so many people," says Tracey. "For me, he reminds me to make the most of life, whatever happens. If my blind dog can embrace life with so much enthusiasm, then so can I. He has massively helped me with my depression and anxiety because he is like a tonic – it's hard to feel down when he's around. I've made so many lasting friendships because of him. I love all my dogs but there isn't one quite like him. I am so blessed to be his mum and I know that I can tackle anything with him by my side. He is such a special little guy who radiates positivity wherever he goes. We might have rescued him, but he has helped so many people. He is a genuine hero. In fact, he's *my* hero and we could all learn about how to live fulfilling lives, no matter what happens, from him. He's an inspiration!"

Chapter 29

AMANDA AND PIPER PAWS THE CAT

Many mothers and daughters are close, but Patricia and Amanda enjoyed a particularly special relationship. Growing up in West Virginia, Amanda was introverted and quiet. She didn't make friends easily and only had a couple of girlfriends she hung out with at school. She was also an incredibly clumsy and uncoordinated child. She would often fall over her own feet or would just collapse for no reason. Her mom Patricia was adept at catching her before she landed on the floor and was protective of her daughter. Visits to her paediatrician didn't offer an explanation for her tumbles, and Amanda spent a lot of time in Patricia's company.

It wasn't until she was 17 years old and suffering from debilitating headaches that a doctor finally ordered a CT scan, which showed up surprising, unexpected results. It revealed that Amanda was suffering from a neurological condition called Dandy–Walker syndrome, a very rare congenital brain malformation, which she had been born with and that had gone undetected. Her falls were in fact symptoms, and explained why Amanda had struggled to walk and had physical therapy until she was two years old. People with Dandy–Walker syndrome are often diagnosed with autism, too, and suddenly the way Amanda had felt for the past 17 years made some sense.

"I lived in the same house with my mom forever," recalls Amanda. "She looked after me and I never wanted to leave her. I did well at school but I had no friends outside – it was just her and me. I was socially awkward, I didn't like to be around other people much at all, except for my mom. I couldn't keep a conversation going with anyone but I was rarely lonely. My balance was an issue. Sometimes I walked like a drunken sailor – many times I fell and got bruised all over my body. I guess we just got used to it and living like that became the normal for me. When I was diagnosed with Dandy–Walker, it accounted for all the symptoms I'd been experiencing my whole life. The disease affected my balance and coordination, and doctors said they believed I also had autism, which accounted for my shy behaviour. They told me that there was no cure and that I had to live with it, so I was sent home. I googled it, saw what it was and I was happy that there was a name for what I was experiencing."

Amanda graduated and married Kenny, a truck driver. They lived with Patricia for the duration of their marriage because of finances and the fact that Amanda wanted to be close to her mom – she wasn't ready to leave. It worked out well, but the couple grew apart and split up in 2004. It was sad but living with her mom helped Amanda to come to terms with her failed marriage and she was fine without Kenny.

Two years later, Patricia started to feel unwell with very heavy periods. She was diagnosed with uterine cancer but after a full hysterectomy her doctors said they had removed all the cancer cells and she was soon declared to be in remission. For years she remained in remission and thrived. Amanda met Adam in 2009 and they eventually got married and again lived with Patricia, who loved having the pair there. Times were good but, in April 2013, Patricia shared some awful news – her cancer had returned, and it had spread to her liver and her lungs.

"Mom told us on the first of April and at first I thought it was an awful April Fool's joke," says Amanda. "She had been so well for many years that the thought the cancer might return never crossed my mind. But she was, of course, serious. I was devastated and it was a very rough time. We found her a new doctor who prescribed chemotherapy, but it didn't work and she died on the nineteenth of April 2014, a year after the cancer came back."

On her deathbed, Patricia made Adam promise that he would get Amanda a kitten. Amanda had recently lost her cat Sprinkles, who she'd had for 16 years and whose death had devastated her.

After Patricia died, Amanda struggled to function. The thought of even leaving the house was too much and her grief tore at her heart to the extent that she wondered how she could ever make it without her beloved mom. Sensing that Amanda was declining, Adam kept his promise to her mother and started to look for a kitten to help fill the massive void that Patricia had left.

One evening in May, not long after Patricia passed away, Adam texted Amanda from the P.U.R.R. animal shelter. A rescued cat had given birth to four tiny black-and-white kittens and Adam had adopted one of the girls for Amanda. Nobody knew much about the poor mom except that she had been picked up off the street and had her babies at the shelter. The kitten was so small she fitted into the palm of Amanda's hand. Delighted with her new friend, she called her Piper Paws, the "Paws" was for her mom – Patricia Alane Warner Spencer.

As soon as Piper came home, a much lighter mood filled the house. Amanda felt more optimistic for the future than at any time since her mom had become ill. Piper attached herself to Amanda right away. If she broke down and cried – which she did frequently in the early days – Piper would snuggle up to her. There was something so soothing about the kitten's cold little nose pressed against her arm or her chest. She would sleep in Amanda's arms all the time and, as she grew, she was funny with her kitten antics. Piper's impression of a bunny around the house always made Amanda laugh and would turn even the worst of days into something better.

"I believe that Piper Paws was sent by my mom to ease my grief and to give me a reason to carry on after she died," says Amanda. "She knew I would need someone special to get me through losing her. Although I had Adam, it was the first time I'd ever been without mom and it was ridiculously hard. I relied on her for so much. She loved me so hard and she was my greatest protector, so she left a gaping hole in my life. Mom knew that Piper Paws would fill that void and she was right. She gave me something to focus on other than my loss. I had to get up every morning to care for my kitten and to make sure that she was okay – I owed it to her not to collapse into my grief."

Piper Paws, now six years old, still enjoys life with her people Amanda and Adam, as well as two other cats, Gandalf the Grey, who is also six years old, and Phineas Nigellus Black, who is four. Together, they live a great life, but Piper is always on hand for love and hugs if Amanda needs them. Piper Paws is also close to Adam now and she rules the roost with the other cats. Being the only girl in the house, she is definitely the princess and she knows it.

"My mom would love her," says Amanda. "She would have picked her out for me. I am glad she told Adam that he had to get me a cat. Even when she was feeling her worst, she was thinking about me and I love her for it. While Piper Paws is here, I feel like I have a little bit of Mom around me. She is incredibly special to me and I'm so glad Adam rescued her. Whenever I feel upset or sad, he puts her on my chest and tells her, 'Do your job,' which makes me laugh every time! Laughing is such a good tonic. I couldn't have chosen a better friend and companion myself."

Chapter 30

MARTHE AND PEGGY THE DOG

The final year of Marthe's English literature degree at the University of Central London was a particularly difficult one. Her living situation wasn't ideal: her boyfriend Josh had a horrible commute every day to work in Cambridge, which saw him get back late and meant the couple didn't get to spend much time together, which was a stress on their relationship. In 2016, she also suffered an awful loss that she couldn't come to terms with. Her best childhood friend, Beth, took her own life. Although Marthe was well aware of Beth's struggles, it was nevertheless devastating.

Marthe and Beth had first met each other in high school when they were 11 years old. They hit it off right away and bonded over their love for dogs. Beth had a lurcher called Belle, who her family rescued from Battersea Dogs & Cats Home in London, and she adored her. Together, she and Marthe, who also had dogs, took their pets for endless walks. While Marthe liked all dogs, Beth was passionate about them.

They left school at eighteen and Beth was one of the only friends that Marthe kept in touch with. They partied together and shared stories of their gap years before they went to university.

"Beth was a wonderful friend. We were very close, even after we left school," says Marthe. "She was an animal lover and her dog Belle was her world. We spent many happy hours walking the dogs and putting the world to rights. Like anyone, she had her demons. She battled with depression and anxiety for many years. She had low self-esteem and she struggled with long-standing issues. When our mutual friend called me to say that she had passed away, it was an absolute shock despite my being aware of her problems. You just never expect anyone to go that far, but I guess she was in more pain than we thought. I was devastated and heartbroken. It was one of the worst times of my life."

Thanks to the support of her university friends, who had met Beth not long before, Marthe consciously put her immense grief to one side so that she could finish her studies. She knew that if she didn't, she would dissolve and wouldn't be able to complete the degree that she had worked so hard for. Somehow, she managed to push through and finish a major thesis two weeks later. She also passed her exams, even though Beth was always in her mind.

In April 2017, Josh suggested that they move to Cambridge so that he didn't have such an awful journey every day.

Marthe agreed but she had one condition – that they adopt a dog.

Growing up, Marthe had been surrounded by dogs. There was an Old English sheepdog when she was a toddler, then a tiny terrier who lived to the old age of 14, and then her parents adopted a cute Jack Russell from the dogs' home. She knew the health and emotional benefits of having a dog and she was ready to make that commitment. Josh agreed and they relocated to Cambridge, where Marthe enrolled in further studies.

At first, she was miserable living in Cambridge. All her friends from university had gone their separate ways so she knew very few people. It was stressful moving to a new place after living so long in a big city. Even after a couple of months and her finding a nice job working for a local charity, she was still unhappy and missed London. They hadn't got a dog yet so she brought the idea up again.

"I told Josh that we were getting a dog," says Marthe. "He said maybe later in the year but I said no, I'm looking now! I wasn't happy. I think that my unresolved grief about Beth came to the fore because my life slowed right down, I didn't like Cambridge and I missed everything about being in London. It wasn't like me to be sad, but I was in a bit of a funk. I needed a distraction and I knew that a dog would change everything for me."

Marthe started scouring local rescue groups for possible pups. There were so many animals that needed homes but one face in particular caught her eye. The dog's name was

Alice and she was thought to be a Mioritic Shepherd Dog. She had been with the Forest Dog Rescue for around six weeks. Her picture was of her looking at the camera with the biggest grin, and Marthe loved the fact that her write-up said that she was a mischievous pup who loved pouncing on people's shoes and untying their laces.

A placement had fallen through, so Alice was looking for a home again and a lot of people were interested in her. Marthe was invited to meet her, but when she walked into her cage, Alice cowered away at first. One of the ladies at the shelter said that the poor dog had come in very anxious and they had worked out a way to pat her without her being scared and flinching. Marthe took her outside in the field for a 45-minute walk and, at the end, Alice let her pat her. Apparently, she had never taken to somebody so quickly, so Marthe was chosen to adopt her.

A few days later, Marthe and Josh went to pick her up. When Josh was meeting her, she heard Marthe's voice and pulled hard to get to her. They took her back to Cambridge and called her Peggy, but it wasn't until they looked in a pet parcel that she had been sent home with that they discovered that she had been rescued from the streets in Bucharest, Romania.

It seemed she had been badly beaten there. It was estimated that the beautiful, fluffy, fawn-coloured girl had been on the streets for several months based on the fact she was so emaciated. One of the ladies at the shelter in Romania where she was initially taken had said that Peggy hadn't wanted to live. She'd cowered in the van, had refused to eat or drink and had been very afraid of men. It had taken a while for them to persuade her to come out and even longer to gain her trust. She was then brought to England to find her forever home.

It didn't take too long for Peggy to settle into life with her new family, although it was three months before she would go near Josh and let him pat her. Marthe was definitely her person from the start. She was still struggling with Beth's death and part of her recovery was a lot of running and long walks with Peggy for company. Together, the pair exercised every day while Marthe trained to run a marathon.

"Peggy was the best running partner," says Marthe. "She's such a bouncy, fun-loving dog and she enjoyed us being out together, on our own. I think she loved the time we spent together as much as I did. We really bonded. If I was sad, she would sit with me, head on my lap so that I could stroke her pretty head. Through tears I would snuggle with her and the feelings of being that close and her unconditional affection was magical. I needed her and she was always there to lift my spirits."

In March 2018, Marthe travelled to Nepal to take part in a 250-km marathon across the Himalayas over six days. She had trained hard for the race and she was excited to compete.

On the second day, halfway up a mountain and all alone, she was attacked by a teenage boy on a hike. He grabbed her and, during the struggle, they fell over a small ledge. The boy tried to strangle Marthe but she managed to fight him off with her metal running pole. She made a run for it and, even though it was all uphill, she didn't stop, except to hide in bushes, and thankfully he didn't follow her.

As she couldn't get hold of anyone for help, Marthe was forced to run 14 km to the checkpoint. People were kind and they helped her, and although absolutely terrified and traumatized, she was safe at last. Despite the attack, Marthe found the strength to carry on and she completed the race.

"I was so proud I managed to finish the marathon," says Marthe. "I have no doubts that the person would have raped and murdered me if I hadn't fought back as hard as I did. It was very frightening, and I remember it was so hard to be running uphill, but I couldn't stop, so I hid in the bushes, cried and carried on. I didn't know that he wasn't going to follow me – in my mind, he was right behind me all the way to the checkpoint. I was always conscious of my surroundings when I ran at home and yet there I was, brutally attacked in one of the safest, most peaceful and spiritual places in the world. The irony of it all was ridiculous."

When Marthe got back to England, it was very difficult for her to get back into her running. Often, if she was in the house alone, she would harness Peggy, get to the front door but then couldn't move, and she would often collapse on the floor. It was the fear and trauma of what had happened to her.

It was interesting that when Peggy got excited to go out for her walk, she would bark loudly as if to tell her mum to hurry up. Yet when Marthe was collapsed on the floor in the hallway, she would be very quiet and cuddle up to Marthe until she was calm and more focused. Marthe would zone out and Peggy would lick her hand or her face to break the freeze and bring her back.

"If it hadn't been for Peggy, I don't think I'd have got my life back after the attack," says Marthe. "She was the biggest comfort to me, more than anyone, and she always knew when I was having a difficult time. Eventually, when I did find the drive to go out and run again, Peggy kept close to me for reassurance. It was hard and it took time for me to get any confidence back, but with her by my side, it was definitely easier. I knew that if anyone attacked me, she would defend me, and I felt safe with my girl. I already knew that we were close, but I think that this event brought us even closer. I couldn't have lived through the trauma without her."

In June 2018, Marthe and Josh moved to Eccles in Manchester and bought a house. It was a big decision moving to an area that has a higher crime rate, especially after having been attacked in Nepal. What could have been a very stressful move wasn't, and it was all because of Peggy.

"Honestly, it would have been easy to have stayed in all the time, particularly if I wasn't with Josh," says Marthe. "But I had to walk Peggy. I had an obligation to her to get out of the house, and with her by my side I wasn't afraid. I was super-cautious all the time, of course, and Peggy knew that."

In 2020, Marthe and Josh adopted another pup from Romania called Rupert. He is a gorgeous white and tan collie–Tornjak cross whose mother wandered into a garden when she was pregnant. Luckily, she chose the garden of a dog-rescue volunteer and the dog's puppies were safely delivered. Rupert, at just five months old, arrived in the UK in the spring and they collected him in April.

He is an absolute bundle of naughty joy who adores his new family. Peggy is most definitely the boss and together they play for hours – she keeps him entertained when Marthe works from home. Not a day goes by when Marthe isn't thankful for both her rescues, who have blessed her life with so much more than she could ever have hoped for.

"Peggy is just an amazing dog," says Marthe. "I'm not sure I would have wanted a traumatized pet but there has been something so precious and beautiful watching Peggy get her confidence and become a happy dog. She gives love on her own terms, so I know that when we cuddle, she means it. Her depth of affection for me knows no limits and knowing that her love is unconditional really puts things in perspective. I owe her so much but she's content with just walking and being next to me. The rescue dog is such a very special animal, and I am fortunate to have two of the best."

Afterword

While I was carrying out interviews and writing this book, there was a pandemic tearing its way across the world. I spoke to people who were cut off from their friends and family due to lockdowns caused by the spread of Covid-19, and each one said that if they didn't have their rescue pets, life would be unbearable.

You see, their pets gave them a reason to get up in the long mornings, to get out and about in the fresh air to walk or to tend to them. They provided much-needed company in times of extreme loneliness, depression and anxiety while we all learned to live in a scary new world.

I would urge anyone to consider taking in an animal in trouble, particularly today when they need us more than ever. Since the pandemic hit and people have lost their jobs, there are more animals than ever before in the shelters or being advertised as needing new homes.

Please don't ever misjudge a rescue pet as being an animal with emotional issues who can't be tamed or trusted. In my research, I've learned that they have perhaps the biggest hearts and the most love to offer if given the chance.

#adoptdontshop

Rescue Pet Resources

There are many animal-rescue organizations around the world doing amazing work, and they are often a good place to start if you are thinking of adopting a pet. Most of the stories in this book were found through rescue groups and here is a compilation of the resources I used in my research. I hope that you will be inspired to adopt an unwanted animal and give it the life it deserves.

Animal Action UAE – search on Facebook or follow @AnimalActionUAE on Twitter

American Society for the Prevention of Cruelty to Animals (ASPCA) – www.aspca.org

Big Cat Rescue – www.bigcatrescue.org

Celia Hammond Animal Trust (UK) – www.celiahammond.org

Chase Animal Rescue and Sanctuary – www.chasesanctuary.org

Cherry Horse Welfare International –
www.cherryhorsewelfareinternational.org

Dark Horse Stables – www.darkhorsestables.net

East Midlands Dog Rescue – www.eastmidlandsdogrescue.org

Humane Rescue Alliance – www.humanerescuealliance.org

Humane Society International – www.hsi.org

My Pig Filled Life – www.mypigfilledlife.org

People United for Rescue and Rehabilitation (P.U.R.R.) –
www.purrwv.org

The Pipsqueakery – www.thepipsqueakery.org

Royal Society for the Prevention of Cruelty to Animals
(RSPCA) – www.rspca.org.uk

Russell's Rescue – search on Facebook

Spaniel Aid UK – www.spanielaid.co.uk

Zambezi Working Donkey Project –
www.zambeziworkingdonkeyproject.org

Acknowledgements

I am so grateful to all the wonderful pet owners who have shared their amazing rescue stories with me. I have enjoyed writing about every single one of you and your adorable rescues and I thank you all for agreeing to inspire others with your inspirational tales of true love and devotion.

I would also like to thank all of my own rescue pets over the years for making our lives brighter and teaching us all exactly what *unconditional* really means. You have all inspired me to write this book and I will be forever thankful to have been lucky enough to call you family. You have brought so much happiness into all of our hearts and I will never forget any of you.

Have you enjoyed this book?
If so, why not write a review on your favourite website?

If you're interested in finding out more about our books,
find us on Facebook at **Summersdale Publishers,** on Twitter
at **@Summersdale** and on Instagram at **@summersdalebooks**
and get in touch. We'd love to hear from you!

Thanks very much for buying this Summersdale book.

www.summersdale.com